Book of Perks

Book of Perks

JAMES R. BAEHLER

An Owl Book

HOLT, RINEHART AND WINSTON
NEW YORK

Library of Congress Cataloging in Publication Data
Baehler, James R.
Book of Perks.
"An owl book."
Includes index.
1. Executives—Salaries, pensions, etc.—United States.
2. Employee fringe benefits—United States. I. Title.
HD4965.5.U6B36   1983b   658.4'072   83-26497
ISBN 0-03-071073-1

First published in hardcover by St. Martin's Press
in 1983.

First Owl Book Edition—1984

Designer: Kingsley Parker
Printed in the United States of America
1 3 5 7 9 10 8 6 4 2

ISBN 0-03-071073-1

Contents

Book of Perks

— 1 —

The World of Perks

A person entering the corporate world soon realizes that those above him enjoy privileges he does not—and the higher the position, the greater the privileges. He can see the assigned places in the parking lot for the company executives and the company-owned cars that fill those spaces. At lunchtime he enviously observes corporate managers at nearby tables as they charge their meals with company credit cards. He watches as his firm's top management periodically goes on a week's retreat to Florida or Palm Springs to ponder weighty matters. When summoned, he is impressed with the size and furnishings of the boss's office and the time his secretary spends on his personal affairs and correspondence. He often must wait at the Xerox machine while an executive's personal documents are being reproduced or at his boss's desk while he finishes a long-distance call to a friend. A trip to the mail room seldom fails to show envelopes and cartons being mailed to children away at school or to acquaintances in other cities. And he senses that behind all the visible manifestations of executive privilege are other, greater, perquisites of office, hidden from view but enticingly imagined.

Corporate perquisites, or perks, are like the stockings you hung up each Christmas for Santa. A few items protrude, but underneath is a host of goodies that can only be guessed at. The purpose of this book is to help you dig down into the pile of goodies to find those you want and to offer some guidelines on getting them and keeping them.

A look around the globe explains why perks exist at all. Visitors to Great Britain gaze in wonder at the swarms of well-dressed businessmen alighting from their Bentleys and entering the hushed foyers of private clubs or expensive restaurants. On weekends the same businessmen are off to the country for grouse shooting or golf. On holiday they stay at the best hotels and frequent extravagantly priced nightclubs. Their suits are from bespoke tailors on Savile Row, their daughters enjoy lavish coming-out parties, and their sons toodle off to Cambridge or Oxford. Given the confiscatory income tax of the British Isles, how is all this possible?

Simply, in any society where the tax rates are onerous, corporate perks are granted to replace the income confiscated by the tax man and to allow for the niceties of life to which those who rise to the top feel they are entitled.

In Japan, the last bastion of the Puritan Work Ethic, perks are made available to virtually all managers. Entertaining is considered part of the job and each manager is expected to wine and dine suppliers and customers three or four times a week. No one questions the chits that are turned in, whether for an evening in a geisha house, a day of golf, or a performance at a Kabuki theater. Since this is the Orient, wives are not included and presumably do not complain.

Even in the ostensibly classless society of the Soviet Union perks are to be found in abundance. The wage differential between workers and managers is deliberately kept small to promote an image of economic equality; high-ranking Soviet officials and industrial managers are paid only a small multiple of a factory worker's wage. But early on, the Soviets realized they had to provide incentives for their ablest people. Soviet perks are reserved for government officials, high-ranking academicians, prominent entertainers, top industrial managers, directors of collective farms, and nondissident intellectuals. Physicians and attorneys are not considered worthy of special privilege (an opinion that many Americans might approve with enthusiasm). Eligible Soviets enjoy spacious apartments in restricted neighborhoods. They shop for luxury goods in stores where the average Soviet citizen is not permitted. Their children are automatically entered into the best schools and most prestigious universities. For relaxation they have country homes provided by the government and take their vacations in Havana or Dubrovnik. Soviet élite are permitted the use of foreign currencies and use them to import clothes, foodstuffs, digital watches, stereo systems and other products from Western Europe. They automatically move to the head of the line in restaurants and theaters, and freely travel about the country in expensive automobiles. Most wondrous of all, traffic is halted as they speed unimpeded through the streets of Moscow and Leningrad. Now that's a perk!

Lest one think public officials in the United States are less imaginative, consider that in 1981 Congress exempted itself from the effects of inflation by indexing its salaries and providing more than $60,000 in untaxed income to cover the "expenses" of each member. Lesser public servants are no less creative, as a personal experience and two stories from the *New York Times* will attest.

One of the benefits of public service in New York City is a pension plan that allows city employees to retire on half pay after twenty years. As it turns out, the pay that is halved is the last working year's total income. Last year, a friend of mine was promoted to a position high in the bureaucracy at the Board of Education. When I congratulated him on his advance he explained that it was only for one year and was solely for the purpose of increasing his pension benefits. He explained that there are a number of positions within the educational system that are set aside for those who feel the need for a larger pension. It is a perk provided by the administration to its members; each year each position is newly filled by an imminent retiree.

Where promotions are not possible because of civil service restrictions, overtime is used to pad the pension benefits. The *Times* described a number of Transit Authority employees who had recently retired on pensions greater than their regular pay. The centerpiece of this story was a Transit Authority police officer who accumulated more than $38,000 in overtime pay in 1981. He promptly retired on a pension of $26,000 a year for the rest of his life, although he had never earned more than $23,000 in annual base pay. All overtime, of course, had to be approved by the employee's superiors, who presumably look upon the arrangement as one of the perks of the job.

In Newark, New Jersey, one simply retires on the job. The mayor of that city found himself in difficulty for arranging to have the chief of security for Newark's water supply perform his duties for the previous seven years while living full time in Florida. When asked about this unusual arrangement, the mayor replied with refreshing simplicity, "I gave him a perk." A grand jury, however, giving no credit for candor, found this explanation less than satisfactory and handed down an indictment for misuse of city funds. A few months later the voters of Newark returned the mayor to office by a substantial majority. And, subsequently, a jury of his peers found him innocent of any wrongdoing.

In Japan, Great Britain, and the Soviet Union the take-home pay of business and industrial managers is considerably less than that of their counterparts in the United States. Yet there is little difference among the lifestyles of comparable-level managers of the four nations. In absolute terms, American managers probably have the edge, but only because the general standard of living is higher in the United States. In relative terms, Soviet managers undoubtedly stand first; they enjoy a lifestyle vastly more congenial than the plodding existence of the average Soviet worker.

In recent years American corporations have awakened to the value of perks and begun to provide them in greater abundance and to managers further down the corporate ladder. Mostly this has been an effort to overcome the effect of inflation, which in terms of real dollars has left many managers in a stagnant financial position. The situation has been worsened by the "bracket creep" effect of inflation, which has pushed many wage earners into the 40- and 50-percent tax brackets. Most married couples find two incomes a necessity, but adding the wife's income to the husband's places many couples in tax brackets they had thought reserved for movie stars and home-run hitters. In addition, the increase in Social Security rates and the raising of the ceiling on which that tax is levied has further reduced real income. Salary increases, like old lovers, are no longer what they used to be.

As a consequence, the benefit of many perks in real dollars is considerable. A company car, for instance, is worth almost $5,000 annually in cash savings, which translates to $10,000 in pretax income for many managers. A low-interest loan provides the opportunity for tax-sheltered investments, which can substantially reduce one's tax liability with little or no risk. Company-paid tuition for college-age children can help prevent middle-class penury during those expensive years.

Once our minimal needs for income and security are filled, if Maslow's "hierarchy of needs" is correct, our attention focuses on a desire for status, prestige, and power, and much of the bumping, jostling, and jockeying of corporate life revolve around the efforts of managers to enhance their status, power, and prestige.

The struggle can range from an effort to secure carpeting for an office to a fierce contest for the position of company president. In either situation, the desire for status is often the primary motivating factor. In many companies, a carpet on the floor of an office marks the step from supervisor to middle manager. A skillful corporate in-fighter will not accept the notion that his job does not warrant an office carpet. He will strive to enlarge the scope of his job, or at least the image of its importance, and thereby qualify for an office carpet. Or he may artfully contrive to have his office moved, knowing that physical space can have a tradition: If the tradition of his office is carpetlessness, it might be best to move to a location that has no tradition. More-over, the installation of carpeting can become a natural part of the move to a different office, causing little of the comment that would occur if carpeting were installed in the old office. A manager who can successfully bring off such a coup has placed himself above the competition and is well positioned for his next move. The monetary payoff is nil, but he has scored an important point in the Status Game.

When two vice presidents compete for the presidency of their company the financial rewards are secondary to the inner pleasure of being The President. At that level, the extra income as president, substantially reduced by infla-tion and taxes, is not as important as the feeling of having won the game and the knowledge that the perks will now be greater. When Michael Blumenthal was president of Bendix Corporation he was quoted as saying: "I don't have a primary interest in money at all. I was making five thou-sand dollars a year as a professor in 1958, and I was thrilled when I got thirteen thousand as the assistant to the presi-dent of Crown Cork." Blumenthal said he was motivated by "the exercise of power."

One might infer that part of the power Blumenthal en-joys is the ability to step into a chauffeured limousine or the company jet and be whisked off to his destination with none of the inconvenience others face in their travels. A few years ago, a division president of a large communica-tions conglomerate was appointed acting group president, responsible for almost one billion dollars in revenue. As acting group president he was entitled to the use of a lim-ousine *mit* chauffeur to convey him to and from work each day. A year later an outside person was brought in as group president and the acting president returned to his previous position as a division president. The company wisely de-cided that after a year of enjoying the comfort of velvet upholstery and the envious stares of the lumpenproletariat, it would be inhuman to ask the man to go back to driving his own car. The chauffeur and limousine were retained and the company kept the services of an effective and useful manager who might otherwise have looked elsewhere.

It is not enough that we know our own worth—others must know it, too. As Brian Moore remarked, "If misery loves company, then triumph demands an audience." Impressive titles, spacious offices, private limousines, photographs in the annual report, and the other elements that constitute the visible symbols of success all serve to confirm the status you have earned. Thus a corporate manager has two tasks: getting the work done and getting the recognition he deserves. Both tasks require full-time concentration, and woe befall the manager who neglects one for the other.

Many managers bury themselves in their work, expecting their superiors to recognize their value and reward them accordingly. However, although it is true that work speaks for itself, it does so in a very small voice. Results cannot always be seen, but image is ever visible and often speaks louder than accomplishment. And much of image is determined by the perks displayed.

An important element in securing proper recognition is acquiring, using, and keeping all the perquisites of office without arousing undue resentment. A deft corporate gamesman is always gracious when seeking advantage, never visibly pushy. His maneuvers are successful because of quiet persistence, not abrasive hustling. He knows what perks are needed to present the best possible image and works diligently but quietly to obtain them.

My first introduction to the world of perks came some years ago when I was preserving our nation's freedom by serving as a private in the military service. Not long after basic training I found myself slumped in a corner of a dingy air terminal at Andrews Air Force Base, waiting for a flight to Europe. Those waiting with me were a fair sampling of our country's military personnel, a mélange of officers and enlisted men. When the plane was finally announced for departure I learned that it would be boarded by rank, highest first. With that announcement a staff sergeant approached, holding the ubiquitous clip board, and approached a stocky, white-haired officer seated at the front of the terminal. The sergeant addressed the officer respectfully. "General Smith, your party can board the aircraft now."

Two majors quickly plucked a mass of suitcases from the floor and hustled out to the plane as the general rose majestically from his seat. Rising with the general and clinging affectionately to his arm was a young woman with an abundance of natural gifts fetchingly displayed in a diaphanous frock. The general placed a proprietary paw on his handmaiden's nearest haunch. "Here's my party!" he said in a voice accustomed to command but with just the right touch of down-home heartiness. The bewitching blond blushed becomingly as the general and the sergeant guffawed together in manly comradeship. This was heady stuff for a lad from a neighborhood where a game of pinochle on an oilcloth-covered kitchen table was thought to be a fast way to spend a Saturday night. All agog, I hurried on to the aircraft when my name was finally called. Alas, my lack of rank had relegated me to a seat in the last row next to the toilet, with nary a glimpse of the general and his odalisque, ensconced in splendor at the front of the plane. Thus did I first encounter the perquisites of power, airily acknowledged in the military as R.H.I.P.: Rank Has Its Privileges.

When Napoleon established the Légion d'Honneur he observed that, "Men are governed by toys." So governments bestow medals on the deserving rich, universities confer honorary degrees on benefactors who fund new gymnasiums, churches have an almost infinite variety of honorary titles for large contributors, and corporations dispense impressive titles and perks as compensation for a sixty-hour work week.

Astute corporate gamesmen distinguish between intangible perks, which confirm their status, such as a corner office or a club membership, and tangible perks, which can be of direct financial benefit, such as a company car or a stock option. A cool head is required to clearly identify a perk provided in place of money and not be deceived into thinking something of real value has been won. The ultimate perk is living well, and that requires real money. The game, of course, is to get all you can of both types of perks so both spiritual and monetary sustenance are obtained. The successful blending of those two goals provides one of the great satisfactions of corporate life.

Salary

Since this book is devoted to the perks of corporate life, it might be helpful to touch upon the greatest perk of all, money. It serves little purpose to work for a company where the perks are abundant but the pay scales are miserly. Actually, high pay usually goes with lavish perks, and low pay usually accompanies few perks. The sensible course, then, is to find a company where the pay is high and where perks will be correspondingly generous.

It is almost impossible to discover the pay scales of a company, but the compensation of its principal officers must be disclosed in proxy statements and 10K reports. The pay of a company's chief executive officer is often a fair indication of the pay levels below him. On that assumption, the following charts may prove helpful in determining choices for preferred employers. Comparisons are provided for ten industries. Within each industry the three companies that pay their chief executive officers the most and the three that pay the least are listed.

LEADING CONGLOMERATES

Company	CEO	1981 Salary and Bonus	Sales in Billions
LTV Corporation	Paul Thayer	$1,164,000	$8.77
Rockwell International	Robert Anderson	1,115,000	7.04
United Technologies	Harry J. Gray	1,025,000	13.67
Greyhound	John W. Teets	359,000	4.70
Honeywell	Edson Spencer	483,000	5.35
3M Corporation	Lewis Lehr	551,000	6.51

Note that Lewis Lehr is responsible for almost the same revenue as Robert Anderson but earns less than half as much. The assumption can be made that a similar pay disparity exists between other managers of the two companies. The difference is certainly not two to one at all levels, but even a 10-percent disparity can add up to a significant advantage for the Rockwell managers over the course of a career.

CHEMICAL COMPANIES

Company	CEO	1981 Salary and Bonus	Sales in Billions
Allied	Edward Hennessey	$788,000	$6.41
Union Carbide	William Sneath	756,000	10.17
DuPont	Edward Jefferson	727,000	22.81
PPG Industries	L. S. Williams	590,000	3.35
American Cyanamid	James Affleck	459,000	3.65
Dow Chemical	Paul Orefice	446,000	11.873

METAL MANUFACTURERS

Company	CEO	1981 Salary and Bonus	Sales in Billions
U.S. Steel	David Roderick	$784,000	$13.94
Republic Steel	William De Lancey	679,000	4.34
Armco Steel	Harry Holiday	664,000	6.91
Bethlehem Steel	Donald Trautlein	556,000	7.30
Kaiser Aluminum	Cornell Maier	545,000	3.22
Inland Steel	Frederick Jaicks	505,000	3.75

PETROLEUM REFINERS

Company	CEO	1981 Salary and Bonus	Sales in Billions
Mobil	Rawleigh Warner	$1,449,000	$64.49
Union Oil	Fred Hartley	1,300,000	10.74
Exxon	Clifford Garvin	1,006,000	108.11
Cities Service	Charles Waidelich	477,000	8.90
Ashland Oil	John Hall	309,000	9.26
Amerada Hess	Leon Hess	200,000	9.32

And you thought every oil company loved to throw its money about. Obviously, some do and some don't. I have the feeling that Leon Hess does not look kindly upon managers seeking the good life through company perks.

PHARMACEUTICAL COMPANIES

Company	CEO	1981 Salary and Bonus	Sales in Billions
Bristol-Myers	Richard Gelb	$860,000	$3.49
Johnson & Johnson	James Burke	655,000	5.39
American Home Products	John Culligan	638,000	4.13
Abbot Labs	R.A. Schoelhorn	458,000	2.34
Merck	John Horan	456,000	2.92
Upjohn	Ray Parfet	405,000	1.89

OFFICE-EQUIPMENT MANUFACTURERS

Company	CEO	1981 Salary and Bonus	Sales in Billions
Xerox	C.P. McColough	$731,000	$8.69
IBM	John Opel	692,000	29.07
Control Data	William Norris	687,000	3.10
Pitney Bowes	Fred Allen	437,000	1.41
Wang Labs	An Wang	357,000	0.85
Data General	Edson de Castro	206,000	0.73

Xerox has always paid well and they continue to do so, even as they continue to lose market share. How long this can go on is a matter of conjecture. Data General is the computer company that plays "hard ball," refusing to follow the gentlemanly practices of most of the industry. Edson de Castro runs a tight ship where sixty-hour work weeks are commonplace and expense accounts are carefully scrutinized.

RETAILERS

Company	CEO	1981 Salary and Bonus	Sales in Billions
Sears	Edward Telling	$986,000	$27.35
J.C. Penney	Donald Seibert	779,000	11.86
Allied Stores	Thomas Macioce	650,000	2.76
ARA Services	William Fishman	428,000	2.91
Supermarkets General	Herbert Brody	376,000	2.99
Safeway Stores	Peter Magowan	375,000	16.58

Don't be deceived by Edward Telling's handsome income. Sears has a long history of low pay and continues steadfastly to follow tradition. However, their employee stock purchase plan has long been one of the best and if you can hang in there for twenty-five or thirty years, you will end up with $300,000 or so in Sears stock.

FOOD COMPANIES

Company	CEO	1981 Salary and Bonus	Sales in Billions
Norton Simon	David Mahoney	$858,000	$3.14
Esmark	Donald Kelly	820,000	3.31
IC Industries	William Johnson	727,000	4.19
Carnation	Everett Olson	385,000	3.35
Campbell Soup	Gordon McGovern	360,000	2.79
Quaker Oats	William Smithburg	347,000	2.59

13

Note that there is no relationship between revenues and CEO pay. This is also true between CEO pay and profits, return on assets, return on shareholder equity, or any other measure of managerial performance.

BANKING AND FINANCE

Company	CEO	1981 Salary	Assets in Billions
First Boston	George Shinn	$950,000	$10.31
Continental Illinois	Roger Anderson	739,000	46.97
Citicorp	Walter Wriston	675,000	119.23
BankAmerica	S. A. Armacost	566,000	121.15
First Interstate	Joseph Pinola	487,000	36.98
Great Western Fin.	J. F. Montgomery	325,000	10.64

As a supplement, here is a list of the top wage earners in American business in 1981 who are not on one of the charts above—and some reasons for their handsome remuneration.

TOP EARNING CEOs, 1981

Company	CEO	1981 Salary and Bonus	Company Profits
Phibro	David Tendler	$2,125,000	$289,300,300
Warner Communications	Steven Ross	1,954,136	226,493,000
Toys "Я" Us	Charles Lazarus	1,223,122	43,700,000
Revlon	Michel Bergerac	1,133,000	174,821,000
Wheelabrator-Frye	Michael Dingman	1,076,000	91,350,000
Ogden Corporation	Ralph Ablon	1,101,000	65,079,000
Northrop	Thomas Jones	1,009,000	47,900,000

If you've never heard of Phibro, you're not alone. Unlike the other companies on the list, they manufacture nothing—nothing, that is, except money. Phibro was formed in the spring of 1981 when Engelhard Minerals and Chemicals Company split into two companies, Phibro (a contraction of Phillips Brothers) and Engelhard Corporation. Engelhard Minerals and Chemicals was a trader of raw materials, primarily gold and other precious metals, and was run as a private fiefdom by Charley Engelhard until his death a few years ago. Charley was supposedly the model for Auric Goldfinger in Ian Fleming's novel *Goldfinger*.

When the company split in two, Phibro took the part of the business that dealt in raw materials and with it 85 percent of the $27 billion in sales. Not long afterwards, Phibro paid $550 million to acquire Salomon Brothers, one of Wall Street's leading investment banking firms. David Tendler now heads the joint enterprise and is in the enviable position of being America's highest-paid CEO.

Managers whose salary and bonus are not yet in six figures can take heart at what awaits them. However, one must sympathize with David Tendler. Two-million-plus is hardly proper compensation for a man whose company had earnings of almost $300 million, at least when Tendler's compensation is compared with that of Thomas Jones. Tendler was responsible for six times as much profit as Jones but only received twice as much income.

A few years ago Steven Ross fortuitously acquired Atari for Warner Communications. Other acquisitions, especially in the record field, did not turn out so well. Fortunately, one acquisition like Atari can compensate for a multitude of errors and in 1981 Atari accounted for more than half the profits of Warner. The company's record earnings brought Ross almost $2 million in pay and more than $19 million in cashed-in stock options. That is not a misprint: In 1981 Steve Ross made more than $21 million in salary, bonus, and cashed-in options.

Charles Lazarus owes his place in the Million Dollar Club to a disaster. The parent company of Toys "Я" Us went bankrupt a few years ago and Lazarus resurrected his division from the ashes. A grateful group of creditors now deny him nothing, as well they should.

The cosmetics industry is famous for giant markups on its

products and pay scales that rival those of international oil companies. There is no essential difference among the products of any of the leading cosmetic companies and success is purely a matter of promotion. Michel Bergerac is continuing in the shoes of the legendary Charles Revson who founded Revlon and taught everyone else how to really move the goods.

There is no sensible explanation for the presence of CEOs from Wheelabrator-Frye, Ogden Corporation, or Northrop in the Million Dollar Club. Boards of directors occasionally act in strange and mysterious ways.

Aside from salary, what perks are available to you? The answer of course depends upon your industry, your company, and your position. Obviously, the higher you stand in your company, the more perks that will be available, but comparable positions in similar companies can have a wide variance in the perks provided. Certain industries are more generous than others in the dispensation of boons. If your company is highly profitable with a satisfyingly upward tilt to the sales curve, the perks will probably be more abundant.

The exception is the profitable company that prides itself on being lean and mean. In such a company the home office is usually a ratty collection of old buildings where the enterprise began; everyone travels economy class; all secretaries are shared; the pension plan and benefits are a joke; and the president carries his lunch in a paper bag. There are no perks except the ultimate perk: big bonuses for performance. You join this kind of company with the knowledge that you are after the big bucks and leaving the good life to others.

Many young companies start out lean and mean and later get fat and complacent. I know an investor in Chicago who has done very well buying stock in small companies, watching them prosper, and selling the stock the day the company breaks ground for its fancy new corporate headquarters. His timing is almost always impeccable. My friend would love a new company named Ethel M. It was founded in March of 1981 by Forrest Mars, the gentleman who founded Mars Candy company and turned it over to his sons some years ago. Ever the entrepreneur, Mr. Mars began the Ethel M company to produce a line of liquor- and liqueur-filled candies. At Ethel M, differences in rank are barely discernible: Everyone (including executives) wears a white uniform; they all punch a time clock; there are no reserved parking spaces; no one has an office; and Forrest Mars lives in an apartment above the plant. Those who work for Mr. Mars have probably never heard the word "perk." Fortunately, for us as managers, rather than investors, other companies know how to properly treat a dedicated executive.

Among the more lavish dispensers of perks are advertising agencies, Wall Street investment houses, movie studios, television networks, nonprofit organizations, public development authorities, and record companies on a hot streak. The Silas Marners of the perks world include insurance companies, farm equipment manufacturers, engineering firms, architects, publishers, food companies, railroads, construction firms, textile companies, and any company connected with the automobile or steel industries. Banks are two-faced: Below the level of senior vice president, you are expected to touch your forelock in humble gratitude for a ticket to a wrestling match; senior vice presidents and above can jet off to Paris for the weekend and nobody will say boo.

The world of perks is complicated by the shifting winds of economic fortune. For two generations automobile executives lived like pharaohs, until the Japanese left them like the statue of Ozymandias, half-buried in shifting sands. Now not only are their perks gone but they are learning to live with pay cuts. In the record industry the reversal happened overnight. In one six-month period in 1979, the ever-ascending curve of record sales flattened and then reversed itself in an equally steep decline. Record company executives whose motto had been "spend, spend, spend" now found themselves doubling up at Motel 6 and asking for receipts at Burger King. There are still some big spenders in the record industry but mostly among smaller companies with hot new rock groups. At CBS, where profits from records and television slumped simultaneously and where William Paley had set a standard of high living which his executives strove manfully to emulate, everyone now travels economy class and group presidents are discovering the virtues of thrift and the ambiance of steerage. Many other companies have taken the pledge and sworn to have no more to do with Demon Spend.

If you are contemplating a change, a thorough investigation of another company's perks is in order. Do not assume that because a company is profitable or in a certain industry that the perks will conform to those in similar companies. There appears to be no correlation between executive compensation, including perks, and profitability. In general, the larger the company, the greater the compensation and the more lavish the perks. This is true even if the company is not as profitable as others in its field.

The best source of information about compensation and perks is the 10K statements and proxy reports that companies must file with the Securities and Exchange Commission as addenda to its annual report. Among other items these supplemental reports list the compensation, in all forms, of principal officers and the cost, if not the nature, of their perks. Needless to say, 10K statements and proxy reports are not distributed with the same enthusiasm as annual reports, which are usually as open and straightforward as a Caribbean travel brochure. If you are a shareholder, a company will provide you with a 10K report, but be prepared for a lengthy wait. Companies are reluctant to part with documents as revealing as a 10K report, so even a stockholder may have to make more than one request. 10Ks are available for examination at the regional offices of the SEC, and some brokerage houses may have a selection.

To aid your investigation a list of possible perks is provided, separated into affinity groups:

CASH IN YOUR POCKET:
1. A signing bonus
2. An annual performance bonus
3. A severance settlement
4. The right to do freelance work on your own time

RELOCATION PROTECTION:
1. Cost of finding a new residence
2. Cost of moving
3. Cost of temporary housing while moving
4. Indirect expenses
5. Mortgage assistance
6. A subsidy to reflect higher living costs
7. Settling-in allowance
8. Unusual costs

PEACE OF MIND:
1. A no-cut contract
2. Company-paid pension plan
3. Paid-up life insurance
4. A paid-up annuity
5. Health-club membership
6. An annual physical examination
7. Personal time
8. Education
9. Consultation with the corporate legal staff
10. Personal security

FINANCIAL LEVERAGE:
1. Stock options
2. Appreciation grants
3. Phantom stock options
4. Formula value grants
5. Low-interest loans
6. Thrift plans
7. Deferred compensation
8. Estate counselling

FINESSING THE TAX MAN:
1. A company car
2. Reimbursement for entertaining at home
3. A liberal expense account
4. Medical and dental coverage

LIVING THE GOOD LIFE:
1. Country club and private club membership
2. Use of the company boat and/or hunting lodge
3. Overseas trips
4. First-class air travel
5. Airline VIP clubs
6. Spouse's travel expenses
7. Frequent-flyer clubs
8. Special hotel accommodations
9. Extra vacation time
10. Sabbatical leaves
11. Tickets to theaters and sporting events

ESTABLISHING YOUR IMAGE:
1. A larger or better office
2. A private secretary
3. A limousine and chauffeur
4. Use of the company airplane
5. Use of the company hotel suite
6. The executive dining room
7. The private dining club
8. A reserved place in the company parking lot

There is your shopping list. How many of these perks do you presently enjoy? Which would you like to have? How should you go about obtaining those you want? Read on and all shall be revealed.

You should approach your quest for perks in the right spirit; these are privileges and comforts to which you are properly entitled. There is no way your company can properly compensate you for the hours you work, the stress you must deal with, and the time you spend away from your family. The perks you acquire can in no way make up for the cost to you and your family of your efforts on behalf of your company. All that perks can do is make your life a bit less arduous. Your company at least owes that to you.

— 2 —

Negotiating for Perks

Consider three corporate managers. Charley is director of advertising for a manufacturer of office equipment. He has been with the company since college and steadily worked his way up the ladder until he is now responsible for an annual advertising budget of $14 million and a staff of six people. He has been in his present position for six years and is highly regarded by his boss. Charley is capable, imaginative, and able to keep his staff working harmoniously as a team. A team player, placing company interests above his personal ambitions, he has labored diligently for the company and has the respect of his peers and subordinates. He has never made waves or demanded privileges. Every company needs as many Charleys as it can find.

Anne has just been promoted to director of advertising for her company. She joined the advertising department four years ago after a successful entry into the business with an ad agency. During the past four years she has taken on tasks of increasing responsibility and has performed well. In her new job she will, like Charley, have a budget of $14 million and a staff of six. Anne was promoted over a man in the department who was also highly regarded. Others in the company had doubts about Anne's ability to do the job and thought the company should have gone outside to fill the position. Anne's boss persuaded them to allow Anne the opportunity to prove herself.

Pete has interviewed for a position as director of advertising with a new company and the personnel manager has told him they are going to offer him the job. Like Charley and Anne he will have a budget of $14 million and a staff of six. Pete made a favorable impression on all those involved in the interviewing process at his new company and his track record in his two previous jobs was good. The personnel director at the new company told Pete that the company president was very pleased with him and was sure he would add a lot to the company. Pete is looking forward to the new job and is confident he will be able to do it well, but first he must work out the salary and other benefits with the company president.

Question: Assuming the three managers decide to go after all the perks they can acquire, who is in the strongest bargaining position, Charley, Anne, or Pete?

If you answered, "Charley," you ought to perhaps think about finding employment with the government or some other large bureaucracy. In terms of perks, Charley is dead in the water. If he really makes a fuss, he might get his office redecorated; that's about it. Mr. Nice Guy has been taken for granted too long. Providing him with perks isn't going to make him work any better or harder, so why bother? His boss will determine what minimum perks are necessary to keep Charley reasonably satisfied and that's all Charley gets. If he becomes too insistent, the boss will start thinking it's time to get some new blood into the advertising department.

If you chose Anne, you can build a stronger case than for Charley, but Anne's position is not much better. Anne's promotion is thought of as sufficient reward; requests for extensive perks are going to receive a cold reception and cause people to think they should have gone outside or promoted the other candidate in the department. Anne's best course is to obtain what perks she can without ruffling any feathers, then let the boss know what other perks she would like and make them contingent upon achieving specific performance goals.

A truth of business life is that another company will always value your services more than your own. Because of that, Pete is about to receive an offer of a new job with a promotion and pay increase that he might never have gotten if he had stayed with his old company. When someone joins a new company all that is visible are his strengths. After a few years the strengths are taken for granted and the weaknesses become more apparent. A similar transformation takes place among couples who marry on short acquaintance and three years later can see only their partner's shortcomings.

The best time to negotiate for perks is just before the "marriage ceremony," when your knightly armor is still unblemished. The second best time is when you have been promoted into a difficult situation that no one else can handle. A computer specialist was recently given his boss's job after the boss had all but paralyzed the company's computer system through mismanagement. The new manager was the only one who understood the system well enough to design and implement a plan of recovery. Realizing the strength of his position, he negotiated a package of perks so extensive they had to be approved by the board of directors.

Pete is in a strong position to negotiate for the perks he desires. However, the negotiations must be concluded before he gives notice at his old job; once that occurs, his bargaining position is much weakened. The bargaining for perks should be part of the negotiation process by which the terms of Pete's employment are worked out. Let's follow Pete as he prepares to bargain with his new employer. Remember, his old company still knows nothing of Pete's plans and, should they fall through, he can continue with his old company as if nothing had happened.

The first task in negotiations is to obtain as much relevant information about the situation and the other side as possible. Pete has used his meetings with the personnel director to learn the general framework of the compensation package the company plans to offer. Pete also wants any other information that will allow him to assess the strength of his bargaining position. For example, if Pete refuses the offer, does the company have an alternative candidate ready to step in? If not, Pete's bargaining position is enhanced. Who is running the department until the new manager arrives? Is that person doing an acceptable job or is the company getting desperate for some effective leadership? How long has the company been looking? Has the job been offered to someone else and refused? How much turnover has there been in the department? Is the present staff experienced and capable or will the new manager have to shoulder most of the burden until the staff can be adequately trained? What salary and perks go with the job in other, similar companies? The answers to these and other questions will help Pete evaluate how much he can ask for during the negotiations and how firm his stand should be. Pete's attitude should convey that he is reluctant to leave his old company but is intrigued by the challenge of the new job. Ideally, Pete should be the wooee not the wooer.

Pete decides his first priority is to obtain the highest salary possible. The personnel manager has told Pete that the starting salary can range from $48,000 to $60,000. Pete is presently making $43,000 and decides he will not change jobs for less than $55,000. He feels he is negotiating from a position of strength. He is happy where he is and can stay there without worrying about fitting into a new company. The personnel manager of the new company has told him that he is the first choice for the job and that the company wants to move quickly to fill the position. If Pete turns down the offer, it will take them a long time to find another suitable candidate. He decides to ask for a high salary and a package of perks that includes the following, in order of priority:

1. A company car
2. An annual performance bonus
3. Three weeks vacation
4. Options on $50,000 worth of company stock

5. A $50,000 loan for five years at 5-percent interest
6. First-class air travel
7. Membership in a health club

Is Pete going to get all that he asks for? Probably not, but he's going to get a lot more than if he waits to be told what perks come with the job. What he must guard against is asking for so much that he is regarded as greedy or unrealistic, or so little that the boss gets suspicious ("If I can buy this guy so cheap, there must be something wrong with him"). Pete will be negotiating with the company president and must evaluate his new boss to assess what the boss can and cannot do within his authority. He must also accurately judge how fervently he is wanted, remembering the call-girl rule: "Something is always worth more before its purchase than after." Once he accepts the new job and delivers his body, his negotiating strength will have all but vanished.

Pete will conduct his negotiations in a spirit of good humor and with an attitude of apparent reasonableness. He will strive to create the impression that he is eager to tackle his new responsibilities but that he must consider his future and his family's well-being in a business-like way. The negotiations might go something like this:

COMPANY PRESIDENT: Pete, I'd like to confirm the information I'm sure you received from our personnel manager; we're pleased to offer you the job of director of advertising.

PETE: Thank you, sir, and I am eager to get to work and implement some of the ideas we discussed in past meetings. Before we discuss my starting date I'd like to come to an understanding about my compensation package. ["I'm not going to commit myself to the job until I know all the details."]

PRES: That sounds like a good idea. Pete, we'd like you to start with a salary of $50,000 per year and, of course, you'll be immediately eligible for our extensive medical benefits and our pension plan. You'll have two weeks vacation and after five years you'll be eligible for an additional week. How does that sound to you?

PETE: To be honest, sir, I had thought your offer might be a bit more attractive. I'm currently making $43,000 and I'm scheduled for a merit increase next month. ["Not true, but there's no way he can check."] On that basis, $50,000 is not enough to persuade me to change companies.

PRES: I see. Well, I'd be interested in your thoughts on a salary that would be attractive to you. But I have to say that we must keep the salary for this job in line with similar positions in the company.

PETE: ["Horsefeathers! There are no similar jobs within the company and, even if there were, I'm not similar to anyone else in the company. If you want to get a top-flight advertising guy you are going to have to pay for it, whether it's me or someone else."] Mr. Jones, I want to emphasize that I consider the job you've described as crucial to the marketing effort of your company. Unless your new director of advertising knows what he is doing, your revenue is going to suffer, no matter how hard the sales force works. Would you agree with that? ["Let's not forget, this is a job that directly affects the sales and earnings of the company."]

PRES: Yes, I would agree with that.

PETE: Fine. Now a job like that should have a salary commensurate with its importance. I think the position warrants a salary of $65,000 a year. ["I'm taking a chance starting this high. He might be put off and look for someone else, but I think he'd prefer to negotiate."]

PRES: Good heavens! Pete, we could never pay that much for a director of advertising. Why, some of our vice presidents don't make that much. We might be able to go a little higher than 50K, but we couldn't approach what you're asking.

PETE: ["What do I care what your vice presidents are making! Your offer of 50K was too low and I countered with a bid that was too high. Now let's bargain!"] Mr. Jones, I like the challenge and opportunity that your company offers, but

$50,000 does not seem adequate for the responsibilities of the position. ["The ball is in your court."]

PRES: Pete, I think I can understand how you feel, and because we do want you with us I think we might be able to start you out at $55,000. How does that sound to you?

PETE: ["It sounds fine to me but I'm not going to let you know it."] Mr. Jones, $55,000 might be acceptable, provided other items were part of the package.

PRES: What other items?

PETE: I've given the matter considerable thought and I'd like to propose this. Since my salary needs could not be met, I would like to have a company car, a loan of $50,000 for five years at 5-percent interest, a $10,000 annual performance bonus, options on $50,000 worth of company stock, three weeks vacation, first-class air travel, and membership in a health club. ["I'm taking a chance that he'll be offended and walk away, but if he does, I can be happy staying where I am. Let's see how badly he wants me."]

PRES: Pete, there's no way in the world we can agree to that list of perks. I realize the salary we offer is not what you were thinking of, but you're just asking for too much.

PETE: ["Of course I'm asking for too much. Now we'll find out how much you're willing to give."] Well, I don't necessarily agree that I'm asking for more than a comparable job would offer at another company, but what do you think would be equitable? ["You do want to be fair about this, don't you? Hardly. You want to buy me as cheaply as possible, but you want to give the appearance of fairness."]

PRES: Suppose we do this. I'll agree to the first-class air travel, the health club, and the three weeks vacation. How does that sound?

PETE: ["It sounds lousy. I want something that puts money in my pocket."] Those items are nice, Mr. Jones, but they are all intangible benefits. I need some items to make up for the $10,000 of salary I agree to give up. ["It's always nice to give up something you never had, especially when it puts the other guy at a disadvantage."]

PRES: Pete, I just don't know how I can offer any more than I have.

PETE: Don't forget, Mr. Jones, if I leave my present company, I lose considerable money that has been placed in a profit-sharing program by my company. If I stay another three years I will be fully vested in that entire amount. ["It only comes to a few thousand dollars so far but, once again, he doesn't know that."] That is why I am asking for the stock options and the loan.

PRES: Pete, the stock options are just not possible; those are reserved for vice presidents and up. I may be able to do something on the loan. Suppose we agree to the loan as you described it—but it would have to be fully paid up at the end of five years.

PETE: That would be acceptable, Mr. Jones. It seems that all we have left to discuss is the performance bonus and the company car. ["I haven't yet put any real money into my pocket."] Let me ask you to consider this: There won't be any relocation expenses involved if I join your company, which may not be the case if you have to find someone else. ["A reminder that he may have to start this whole process over again ought to shake him up a little."] I know you've tried to be equitable during our negotiation and I appreciate that. I want to be reasonable about this also. You'll be saving money on relocation expenses, and I need some cash to make up for the lower salary. I won't insist on both the performance bonus and the company car. I'll let you decide which one I should have. ["It's a forced choice. Heads I win; tails you lose."]

PRES: Pete, the performance bonus is out of the question. If I provided it for you, every manager in the company would be after me for the same benefit. Perhaps I can authorize a company car on the basis that you need to travel quite a bit to meet with our sales people and the ad agencies we do business with. I'll see that you get the car if you'll agree to all the other parts of the package.

PETE: ["Congratulations, you finally made an offer of

yours contingent on my doing something. Your negotiating skills are improving, but it's a little late."] That would be fine, Mr. Jones. We've got ourselves a deal. Let me just summarize to make sure we're clear on the details. The starting salary is $55,000 a year. In addition, I receive the use of a company car, a $50,000 loan at 5-percent interest payable in full at the end of five years, three weeks vacation, first-class air travel, and membership in a health club.

PRES: You know those last two items may cause some problems. I think we need some guidelines there. I would ask that the first-class air travel be restricted to flights of two hours or more and that the health club fee not exceed $500 per year.

PETE: That is fine with me, Mr. Jones. I am looking forward to starting with your company just as soon as possible.

PRES: Pete, we're glad to have you with us, and if you do your job as well as you've negotiated today, we're all going to be very happy.

PETE: Thank you, sir.

Aside from Pete's successful effort to secure the salary and perks he wanted, the most interesting aspect of this type of negotiation is that both sides develop respect for one another. Pete has learned that his new boss values Pete's services and is willing to listen to reason when presented with reasonable arguments. The boss has developed respect for Pete's business acumen, for knowing the value of his services and not settling for less. Each party knows the other is serious about his work and is not hesitant to protect his legitimate interests. The basis for a mutually satisfying business relationship has been established.

It is also interesting to note that while Pete didn't get all he asked for, he certainly got much more than he was offered initially. If Pete had gotten all he asked for then he hadn't asked for enough. If he didn't get anything above the initial offer then either the company didn't want him very badly or he is a poor negotiator.

Let's not ignore salary, the most important and useful perk of all. If your first priority is more income, think seriously about changing companies. Unless you are being promoted every two or three years, it's probably time to move on. Look around; you may be surprised to discover what someone is willing to pay to win you away from your present employer. You ought to figure on a salary improvement of 25 percent or more to make a move. How long will it take you in your present job to raise your salary by that amount? And remember, any increase becomes the base for future increases; its effects are compounded far into the future.

Now that you know how to negotiate for your perks, the question arises as to where you should practice your new skills. If you stay in your present job, you will have limited opportunity to obtain new perks, at least until your next promotion. Nevertheless, you may be interested in knowing which specific companies provide more perks and which provide less. Even if you are not planning an immediate change, it doesn't hurt to have an idea of where the goodies are abundant and which companies Santa never visits.

Let's assume that the perks provided to a company's CEO are a reasonable indicator of those provided to other managers in the same company. On that basis the following list of companies and the value of the perks provided to their CEOs should prove helpful. For this listing, perks include all forms of cash-equivalent compensation, such as club dues or insurance premiums, use of a company car or airplane, stock bonus awards, thrift-plan contributions, restricted stock awards vested or released from restrictions, and other fringe benefits. Not included are travel or entertainment expenses, counseling by corporate attorneys or accountants, extra vacations, office renovations, tickets for theater or sporting events, low-interest loans, and other perks that can be buried among the company's operating expenses and need not appear in a 10K report or a proxy statement. The listing therefore should be seen as a guide and not a definitive statement on CEO perks.

Company	1981 CEO Perks	1981 Profits
Heublein, Inc.	$591,000	$ 88 million
Phibro (what, again!)	543,000	289 million
G.D. Searle	494,000	99 million
Holiday Inns	443,000	137 million
Standard Oil California	369,000	2.3 billion
Freeport-McMoran	362,000	159 million
Cooper Industries	357,000	284 million
Reading & Bates	334,000	N/A
Baker International	328,000	225 million
Mesa Petroleum	317,000	115 million
American Standard	306,000	111 million
IBM	301,000	3.3 billion
Sundstrand	298,000	95 million
Allegheny International	255,000	81 million
Scientific Atlanta	253,000	19 million
Parsons	252,000	N/A
Norton Simon	241,000	103 million
Cameron Iron	234,000	110 million
United Technologies	210,000	457 million
Boeing	203,000	473 million

There are some interesting anomalies above. Leading the perks list is Hicks B. Waldron of Heublein with almost $600,000 in 1981 benefits, although his company's profits of only $88 million rank it second from the bottom on that scale. One can only wonder what the Heublein board of directors sees in Mr. Waldron that is lost on those who study the company's profitability. Perhaps they were anticipating the merger in which Heublein became part of R.J. Reynolds.

One might wonder whether the same board serves at Heublein and at Scientific Atlanta ($19 million in profits), where Sidney Topol dipped into the goodie bag to the tune of $253,000—only a few steps below John Opel of IBM ($3.3 billion in profits). On IBM's profit and loss statement

$19 million would be lost in rounding off to the nearest $100 million. Perhaps Topol is being rewarded for having the courage to head a high-tech company not located in Silicon Valley or along Route 128 near Boston.

G.D. Searle's profits of $99 million would hardly seem to qualify Donald Rumsfeld for perks worth almost $500,000, but he is a special case. Rumsfeld joined Searle after serving in Nixon's cabinet as secretary of defense. Any stint in the nation's capital, no matter how brief, will develop a taste for the good life, and duty at the higher levels of the Pentagon often creates a permanent penchant for the pork barrel.

Which brings us to the list of naughty companies whom Santa never visits. These are companies who provide no visible perks to their CEOs, no contingent remuneration, and no stock gains realized in 1981. The CEOs of these miserly organizations must content themselves with a simple salary and bonus. The shareholders are undoubtedly pleased with this state of affairs, but one can only wonder at the ascetic spirit which motivates the CEOs. Self-denial is a worthy principle but there should be limits to it. After all, hair shirts have never been found in fashionable men's stores. Be that as it may, here is the list of corporate orphans for whom Christmas never comes:

Company	CEO	1981 Salary and Bonus
Armstrong	Harry Jensen	$322,000
Avco	Robert Bauman	316,000
Chrysler	Lee Iococca	362,000
Crane	Thomas Evans	403,000
Evans Products	Monford Orloff	593,000
Libby-Owens-Ford	Don T. McKone	275,000
Northwest Airlines	Joseph Lapensky	325,000

Company	CEO	1981 Salary and Bonus
Overseas Shipholding	Morton Hyman	$360,000
Pantry Pride	Grant Gentry	319,000
Polaroid	William McCune	325,000
Singer	Joseph Flavin	483,000
Tecumseh Products	Kenneth Herrick	170,000
Woolworth	Edward Gibbons	400,000

In addition to the above list there is a multitude of banks, insurance companies, and utilities that also do not provide visible perks to their CEOs—so many of them that it would have been impractical to list them. Such additions would have also been deceiving in that those organizations are past masters at hiding the actual perks received by their CEOs. However, they would certainly qualify for the list of Santa's orphans, at least as far as managers below the senior vice president level are concerned.

If you decide to stay where you are, all is not lost. Take your list of desired perks and decide which you would like to have the most. You will then have your objectives. Now, how do you go about achieving them? It's time to make a plan. Perhaps all that is required is a heart-to-heart talk with the boss. If you and he are simpatico, a simple presentation of your case may do the trick; if he has the authority, he may grant your wishes. Perhaps more is involved, however. If the permission of someone else is required, how is it best to appeal to that person? You and your boss should work out an approach that takes into consideration the person and the political factors involved. Develop your plan in detail and put it into action.

If your boss is unsympathetic, the only way you are going

to enjoy more perks is to be in a job with a higher classification. You have two choices: Get your own job reclassified, or get promoted. Getting promoted is something you are probably already actively working on. While you are waiting for your promotion, get to work having your present job upgraded. Again, you have a choice of two approaches: Reorganize the department so it appears as if you have more responsibility, or actually take on more responsibility. With either course, once the changes have been completed, sit down with your boss and work out the best approach to the personnel department on getting your job reclassified. Remember, the personnel department is not going to resist a change that is supported by the heavyweights in the company. Try to get either formal or tacit approval from those above your boss as high as you can go. You want to deal with the people in personnel from a position of strength, not as a humble supplicant.

By and large, personnel managers are bureaucrats; they don't like to make decisions and they respond best to pressure from above. If your plan is to succeed, you will need some artillery behind you when you confront the personnel department. When you have succeeded, no gloating! Thank the personnel folks for their help in your most sincere manner. Don't give them a cause for resentment.

Now that we know what perks are available and have some insight into how to obtain them, let's look at some of the forces standing between you and the good life.

— 3 —

The Forces of Evil

On the surface, the Perks Game appears to be a one-sided contest, with the opposing team fearsome in its invincibility. Surveying your opponents, you may feel George Plimpton's terror when his fragile body was confronted by the defensive line of the Detroit Lions. But do not despair. Plimpton survived and prospered and so will you, if you recognize your own strengths and the inherent weaknesses of the other side. Arrayed against you are the company auditors, the Internal Revenue Service, your corporate peers, occasionally your subordinates, often the U.S. Congress, frequently the federal courts, and sometimes your boss.

Even the Securities and Exchange Commission can involve itself in your perks, as the Telex Corporation discovered. The SEC staff decided that Telex was not following accepted procedures in accounting for the noncash benefits provided its CEO, Roger M. Wheeler, under the terms of its employment contract. The contract allowed Mr. Wheeler virtually unlimited personal use of the company's staff and facilities, but the SEC felt that even those generous guidelines had been exceeded. The SEC claimed that Mr. Wheeler had charged to the company personal travel expenses for him and his family, advertising costs for other companies in which Mr. Wheeler had an interest, and premiums on a host of personal insurance policies. In his role as CEO, Mr. Wheeler examined and approved his own expenditures with no other auditing control; the SEC thought this procedure might be subject to abuse. The commission also cocked an eyebrow at the provision in Mr. Wheeler's contract that required him to spend no more than half the normal working time on Telex business. Why the SEC should look askance at this perk is somewhat of a mystery; many government employees enjoy the same privilege, albeit on a less official basis. Following Mr. Wheeler's death, Telex agreed to a review of its accounting procedures, and the SEC presumably sent its perks-hunters off on another trail.

What chance do you have against an opposing team that includes agencies of the U.S. government, the federal courts, and your company auditors? Actually, quite a good chance, but only if you follow a few simple principles:

> Strength is weakness
> The pivot must be firm
> The meek shall inherit

An explanation is required? Here it is.

Strength Is Weakness

The forces massed against you are overwhelming in numbers and resources. That is their strength and their weakness. In order to function they have promulgated rules and regulations, issued decrees and decisions, and created forms, questionnaires, and manuals. With so many agencies and individuals competing to control your activity, there is duplication, inefficiency, procrastination, bureaucratic bungling, procedural requirements, and the blessings of red tape. To acquire your perks requires not brute strength but cunning. The enemy cannot be overwhelmed by muscle; it must be made impotent by wiliness.

The style of the successful perks player is calm, unhurried, and displaying a placid countenance. The first step in the Zen style of perks playing is to know the opponent.

Who is your primary foe? Who are the secondary foes behind him? In practical terms this means knowing the answers to the following questions about each perk you wish to acquire:

A. Which government regulations and company restrictions apply?
B. Who, within the company, must you satisfy?
C. What is that person like?
D. What documentation must you provide?
E. What additional records do you need to protect yourself?

Let's say you are the director of manufacturing for a medium-size subsidiary of a four-billion-dollar conglomerate. The corporate rule is that only vice presidents and above may travel first class on business trips. The government restrictions in this instance are nonexistent and all you must concern yourself with are company regulations. You want to travel in the comfort of first class and for the opportunity to meet people who might be helpful to you in your career. (Many a chance meeting between seatmates has resulted in benefits to both.)

You investigate the company regulation further and discover there is an exception to this rule, as there is to most. Persons other than vice presidents may travel first class if there are no coach seats available when the reservation is made. Now your course is clear; you make your reservation the day before the flight, not two weeks in advance. With the reduction in flights because of the mass firing of air-traffic controllers and the plethora of discount air fares, the chances are good that only first-class seats will be available, and you will soar off to your destination, warmed by the proximity of other successful business persons and basking in their acceptance of you as one of them.

Upon your return you submit your expense sheet and are surprised to have it bounced back with a question mark next to the air fare. You scribble a note that only first-class seats were available and send the sheet back. It is returned asking for proof that only first-class seats were available. What do you do next? Trying to get a letter from the airline proving your case will be a drawn-out affair and probably fruitless. If you do succeed in demonstrating that only first-class seats were available, you are probably going to get a sharp memo telling you to plan your trips in advance so that future first-class travel is not necessary.

All problems could have been avoided by remembering the necessity for documentation. If the reservations had been made with a trusted travel agent, he would have happily provided you with a letter to be submitted with your expense sheet stating that only first-class seats were available. In fact, even when coach seats are available, your friendly travel agent will provide you with a letter stating otherwise. Why shouldn't he? He keeps your business; the higher priced ticket increases his commission; and who can prove that coach seats really were available? With a proper letter submitted with your expense sheet there may be some grumbling from a corporate auditor, but auditors are always grumbling and a bit more isn't going to hurt.

The strength of your opponent is in the regulations he enforces and his authority to demand documentation from you. You turn that strength into a weakness by uncovering a loophole in the regulations and by providing documentation to support your position. Once a document is submitted, it must be accepted as genuine until proven otherwise. The burden of disproof is on the auditor; when you have submitted a document you feel meets the company requirements, do not be pressured into supplying additional proof. Auditors are notorious for demanding ever more evidence from their victims. Once you get into that demand/response situation, there is no end to it until the auditor wearies of the game or you agree to remove the charge from your expense sheet. If your initial document seems to satisfy company requirements, let it stand. If you are patient and coolly deflect the auditor's blows, you will win. At that point you bow graciously and retire from the arena.

What can be learned from this brief scenario? First, the rules must be known so that they can be turned to advantage. Second, documentation must always support your position. Third, outside assistance from someone like a travel agent, a maître d', or a club manager is often helpful.

The last point requires further elaboration. In any struggle, allies often mean the difference between victory and defeat. To win the Perks Game, you should develop dependable allies, both within the company and without. It is even possible to make an unwitting ally of the company auditor. Get to know the person in Accounting who reviews your expense sheets. Make the approach on the basis that you want to save his time and yours by knowing the correct procedures for submitting your expense sheets. Ask him how you can make his work easier. Would he like the expense sheets typed so they can be read more easily? Does he have a preferred format for the sequence of receipts? Should you identify the items on your hotel bill so that he doesn't have to puzzle them out? Take an interest in his problems and give him what he needs to make his job easier. If you do, your expense sheets will receive only cursory attention; the auditor will spend his time scrutinizing expense forms from those less considerate.

An alternative ploy is to submit your expense sheets for several months at a time with all the receipts jumbled up and with the forms completed in splotched ink, with numerous erasures and corrections. If your accounting department is overworked and the manager is not a stickler for absolute accuracy, your sheets may be accepted simply because no one has the time or motivation to dig through them. Again, strength becomes weakness.

There are other allies we will meet in later chapters, but a further word should be said about travel agents. A knowledgeable and cooperative travel agent can be of enormous benefit to a corporate perks player. He can provide the documentation needed to fulfill corporate regulations regarding travel; he can obtain airline and hotel reservations when space is supposedly not available; he can make it possible for spouses to go along on business trips at minimum cost, and he can play with the everchanging air fares to your personal advantage. If you have been dealing directly with the airlines and hotels or using the corporate travel department, stop now. Find a travel agent who is capable, cooperative, and efficient. Explain your situation and travel needs and enlist his support. He will be happy to have your business and will go out of his way to accommodate you.

I know one middle-level manager who frequently flies cross-country. He always travels by the cheapest night flight or discount fare. His travel agent provides a bogus ticket showing the regular air fare and the manager pockets the difference of $300 or so. This is not a recommended course of action but an indication of the lengths to which travel agents are willing to go to keep a valued customer.

The Pivot Must Be Firm

In your acquisition of perks, the pivot upon which your quest must balance is your boss. If he is opposed to your efforts, there is little hope of success. He is too close to you to be neutralized by red tape or the use of exceptions to rules. His opposition will be fatal to your plans; if his support cannot be won, then he at least should not oppose your efforts. The best solution, of course, is to have your boss in favor of your activities and firm in his support of you. How can this be done?

To win your boss's support, you need to focus on his needs rather than on yours. How can he benefit by your acquisition of corporate perks? The simplest solution is to convince him that the perks you seek will make you a happier, more effective employee. In effect, you are negotiating the perks you want for the productivity he wants. The best approach is a frank discussion with your boss as to what your objectives are and what you will give in return for his support.

Richard is a friend of mine who had outstanding success as a salesman for a company that manufactures industrial coatings and finishings. He is a hard worker who never objected to the considerable travel his job required; in fact he enjoyed it. He has a direct, no-nonsense manner that men and women respond to and that helped him establish quick rapport with the brisk, let's-get-the-job-done plant managers who were his customers. Some years ago he was offered a promotion that involved the supervision of seven other salesmen. There was a modest salary increase, but Richard did not feel it offset the loss of the freedom he had enjoyed as a top salesman. Richard finally agreed to the promotion on the understanding that his boss would never question an item on any expense sheet that was submitted. The boss agreed so long as the sales team met its quota each year. That was the basis for a long and mutually profitable relationship. The boss benefited from a productive sales team and Richard benefited from a virtually unlimited expense account. Over the course of fifteen years Richard lived in a style that many corporate vice presidents would find hard to emulate. He played golf two or three times a week at the nation's finest courses, always drove a full-sized new car, and stayed at the best hotels. He lived in kingly style with only a modest taxable income to show the IRS. At a comparatively young age, Richard took an early retirement and departed for California to be closer to the golf courses on the Monterey Peninsula and the gaming tables in Nevada. He resides there now, a happy man and living testimony to salutary effects of a liberal expense account.

One must remember that Richard's success was founded upon two pillars: the productivity of his sales team and the support of his boss. The company auditors occasionally complained about the amount of Richard's expenses, but the boss always stoutly defended his subordinate, and the auditors were forced to move on to less strongly defended positions. The pivot stood firm.

The Meek Shall Inherit

Thorstein Veblen in *The Theory of the Leisure Class* discusses the tendency of wealthy people to engage in "conspicuous consumption." He describes how many of the rich feel a need not merely to spend their money but to spend it in outrageous and spectacular ways. Palatial mansions costing millions of dollars are built; tens of thousands of dollars are spent on a single party; ten-million-dollar yachts are filled with notables and sailed through the Greek isles; and the women of the rich are adorned with the most costly jewels and furs.

Inheritors of "old money" and rock stars can afford to be indiscreet in the enjoyment of their privileges, but in the corporate world a conspicuous consumption of perks will often lead to a loss of those privileges.

To go back to a previous example, suppose our director of manufacturing arranged matters so that he traveled first class on every flight he took? Not even the most stouthearted boss could fend off forever the complaints of the auditors; at some point the manufacturing director's travel activities would become a point of discussion between his boss and his boss's boss. The inevitable result would be a curtailment of the manufacturing director's freedom to make his own flight plans. In all likelihood, other privileges would also be looked at and perhaps curtailed. All could have been avoided by a discreet use of the perk of first-class air travel. On short flights, the slight benefit of first-class seating does not outweigh the harmful consequences of overusing the privilege.

Sometimes it is the most inconsequential act that can cause the wrath of the auditors to fall upon an employee. Some years ago I knew a very successful sales manager, Herb, who had been massively padding his expense account with nary a question raised. A dynamic fellow with an aggressive moustache, Herb had an ability to play with his expense account that compared favorably with Heifetz and his violin and provided the wherewithal for the purchase of, among other things, a sizable powerboat. The boat required fuel for its operation, of course, and Herb included the fuel receipts for the boat along with his gas receipts for the company car. One bleak day a sharp-eyed accountant noticed that some of the gas receipts were from the Norwalk Cove Marina. The accountant called the marina and learned their fuel pumps were at the end of a dock and not reachable by automobile. With a diligence bordering on fanaticism, the accountant went back over Herb's expense forms for the preceding nine years and circled all questionable items: gas receipts, restaurant charges, entertainment expenses, etc. The documents were laid before the vice president of finance and subsequently brought to the attention of the vice president of sales. Herb was asked to explain each of the hundreds of circled items but his responses were less than satisfactory. He was given a choice of paying back thousands of dollars in questionable charges or resigning. He wisely chose resignation.

To advance in the corporate hierarchy you need to acquire all the perks to which you are entitled. To stay in the hierarchy, the perks must not be abused. As in the military, rank has its privileges but also its responsibilities. The general flying to Europe and ostentatiously flaunting his traveling companion was running the risk that his behavior would come to the attention of a higher-ranking general whose view of the incident might be less than understanding. A corporate manager who abuses the privileges of his position may find that his services are no longer required or that perks once bestowed can be reclaimed.

When Robert Six was deposed as president of Continental Airlines and kicked upstairs as chairman, one of the major objections to his stewardship was his use of corporate funds and facilities for lavish personal entertaining. As long as Continental Air's revenues and profits showed healthy gains each year, Six was invulnerable. Unfortunately, Continental, along with many other airlines, experienced a downturn, and the board of directors could no longer ignore Six's expenditures.

The seductions of corporate power are many and it takes a sturdy spirit to withstand the siren song of success, which is why the most consistently successful companies play down the perks of their top executives. The privileges of an IBM group vice president are almost unlimited as long as they are exercised discreetly. Even the oil companies have learned to keep a low profile, at least in public. The wise corporate manager knows that the trick is not simply to acquire the perks of power but to hold on to them and to use them wisely.

The fact is that auditors, accountants, and IRS agents are, like the rest of us, seeking the easiest way to do their jobs and searching for maximum recognition in return for their efforts. They are vast in number but so are the files they handle. As in other ways, their strength is their weakness. They have files on all of us but they can only give full attention to very few of them. The files they focus on are those that cry out, "Look me over! I'm not what I seem!" Those cries are heard from files that do not have proper documentation, whose receipts and charges do not match exactly, in which company policy is violated without justification, and whose employees are known to abuse their privileges. No accounting staff can be large enough to carefully scrutinize every expense and every document in every file. A choice must be made as to where their efforts will be concentrated. Be unobtrusive but helpful; always provide supporting documentation and the lads in the green eyeshades will look elsewhere for their prey. The meek shall inherit.

—— 4 ——

Cash in Your Pocket

How pleasant it is to have money, heigh-ho!
How pleasant it is to have money!
Arthur Hugh Clough

There are a number of ways to keep score in the Business Game but annual income is the primary basis on which winners and losers are designated. Most of us feel that the more money we make, the more successful we are. In addition, for most of us success is not something enjoyed in secret; to savor success fully we must know that others are aware of our status and, ideally, envious of it. To leave no doubt in the mind of the beholder we drive expensive automobiles and live in fancy houses; the millionaire who eschews the good life is thought to be slightly daft. Most of us are eminently equipped to enjoy money; the difficulty is in acquiring and keeping it.

Corporate salaries, except at the very highest levels, have the nettlesome habit of lagging just behind needs. At one time I thought this phenomenon a quirk of economics and human nature. The chief financial officer of a major corporation set me straight; a well-designed salary structure provides just a bit less than the employees at each level can be expected to need. The purpose is to motivate everyone to work harder and move up to the next salary level. The reality for corporate managers is that money problems will continue until that happy time when the kids are out of school, the orthodontist has been paid off, and the mortgage has been burned. Until then, with the exception of the chosen few occupying CEO suites, money problems will be a concern for all of us. Fortunately, in the world of perks there are other sources of corporate cash available to us than a straight salary.

A Signing Bonus

Are you taking your talents to a new employer? Are they happy to have you and are they going to pay you a good salary? Excellent, I'm glad to hear that. Tom Wyman was in that enviable position when he moved from Pillsbury to become president of CBS Inc. In fact, the company was so glad to have him that, as the *New York Times* reported, Wyman received a bonus of $1 million upon signing the agreement. (Such a warm feeling comes from knowing you're really wanted.) Archie McCardell must have felt very warm indeed when International Harvester wooed him away from Xerox; Archie got $1.5 million for signing. (Harvester got a CEO they dumped five years later; warm feelings seldom last long these days.)

The signing bonus has become common at the upper levels of management. Apparently, corporate presidents have decided that if athletes are entitled to signing bonuses, so are America's industrial leaders. Charles Acker left Air Florida to become chairman of Pan American World Airways and, aside from other emoluments, received as a signing bonus a one-time payment of $250,000. Robert P. Bauman went to Avco as CEO and, according to proxy material distributed at the annual meeting, received "one-time payments" of $16,000 and $75,000. (How a "one-time" payment can be made twice is a matter for semanticists to decide.) In 1981 Pan Am had an operating loss of $231 million and Avco's earnings fell more than 50 percent. Presumably, the two companies feel that if their new CEOs can reverse those trends, the bonuses will be well worth it.

Do not feel you must wait until you are hired away as a

47

chairman of the board to belly up to the trough where signing bonuses are dispensed. Carl Menk of Boyden Associates reports that in 1981, 15 to 20 percent of his firm's middle-management searches resulted in a signing bonus. The *Wall Street Journal* tells of a textile executive who was offered a $50,000 bonus to sign with a competing firm. Sometimes, the bonus is necessary as the final clincher in a job switch. A vice president of human resources required a cash bonus of $12,000 to make his decision. An office products vice president needed $15,000 of upfront money to persuade him to sign.

Executive recruiters report that bonuses are more common in the South and Southwest but are being paid in all parts of the country when a company feels a manager can make a significant difference in profits. The bonuses can be upwards of $1 million for a CEO or in the $8,000 to $15,000 range for a prized middle manager. Managers most in demand are petroleum engineers, computer specialists, and marketing hot-shots. Others need not despair: Managers in finance, advertising or production can command a bonus if they are wanted badly enough and if their track record inspires confidence. One thing is certain: No one ever received a bonus without asking for it.

How do you ask for a bonus without appearing greedy or creating the impression you are an egomaniac? The simplest and best course is to describe in detail the benefits you would surrender if you left your present company; place a dollar value on the lost benefits and ask for a signing bonus to make you even. It is unlikely your new employer will have accurate information about your benefits, so there is little risk in exaggerating their extent and value.

Your request might go like this: "Mr. Jones, I'm happy we've agreed on the starting salary and the other parts of the compensation package, but there is one other matter that needs to be resolved. I've been with my present company for almost five years and during that time I have accumulated substantial sums in my pension and profit-sharing plans. If I join your company I will lose all my accumulated pension benefits and 40 percent of the amount in my profit-sharing account. I sat down with my accountant and went over this situation and he determined that my net loss will amount to $24,300. I think that is a substantial penalty to pay for leaving my present position. I am sure that neither you nor your company would expect me to absorb that loss, so I would suggest a one-time payment of $24,300 to balance my financial condition. That seems only fair, don't you agree?"

Mr. Jones may or may not agree, but there's certainly no harm in asking. If the request is made in the context above, it is hard to imagine anyone taking offense. You may very well get your signing bonus, or you may only get part of what you ask for, but whatever you receive will be more than you would have gotten without asking. And, if nothing else, should the company refuse to pay anything, you gain insight into how valuable they feel you are or aren't, and how badly they want you or don't.

An occasional problem arises when a bonus of, let's say, $8,000 is paid and the person receives a salary increase of $8,000 the next year. Financially, he has stood still from one year to the next and might feel unhappy that he has not improved himself. To avoid future dissatisfaction, you should look upon your bonus as a gift from Santa and use it accordingly; it should not be incorporated into your thinking as part of your job compensation.

Why don't companies simply pay higher salaries and avoid the problems that bonuses often create? (If present employees learn that a new manager received a bonus, resentment is almost sure to follow.) There are a number of reasons. First, a higher salary might be beyond the range set for the position, creating problems with the personnel department. Second, future pay increases will be computed on a percentage of the base salary; a higher base will produce larger yearly increases far into the future. Third, a cash bonus is a powerful, immediate inducement when a company is seeking to persuade a manager to make a change. Fourth, a bonus provides a competitive edge when two companies are vying for the same manager.

An Annual Performance Bonus

Why do so many job switches occur in January and February? In most companies, in order to qualify for the year-end performance bonus you must be on the payroll as of December 31. If you leave before that, the company is not obligated to pay you the bonus you earned, unless you have a special agreement to receive a pro rata share of your bonus based on the departure date.

Performance bonuses can have two different bases on which their computations are determined: your personal accomplishments or total company results. The ideal situation is to participate in both plans. Then, if you do well but the company stumbles, you still make money. Conversely, if your personal results are not what was expected but the company does well, you again make money. If you hit both numbers, it's off to Hawaii with the wife and kiddies!

Bonuses are awarded on the theory that they motivate managers to work more productively than they ordinarily would. There is a lack of hard data to support this theory, but that is a matter of concern for stockholders, not managers.

In many companies, annual bonuses can amount to 50 or even 100 percent of a manager's base salary. At the upper levels, bonuses are often referred to as "Golden Handcuffs." The potential payoff can be so large that a manager is very hesitant about making a job change. Remember Charles Acker who moved from Air Florida to Pan Am? In 1982 his base salary was $350,000, but there was also a bonus schedule that ranged from a minimum of $100,000 to a maximum of $750,000. At that level there is only one basis for determining a bonus; the CEO's individual accomplishments are synonymous with company performance.

There are some dangers surrounding performance bonuses of which you should be aware. First, many companies use them to justify low salaries. "Don't worry, Charley. At the end of the year when that big bonus comes in, you'll be way ahead of the game." What if (gasp! shudder!) the big bonus doesn't come in? You are the one who suffers, not the company. Do not accept a bonus plan unless it comes on top of the normal salary for the job.

Second, the bonus can be so circumscribed by qualifying phrases that your chance of a payoff would be better in a crap game run by Nathan Detroit: "Bonus shall be paid in the event sales achieve a minimum increase of 16.4 percent, and before-tax revenue increases at least 20.6 percent (excluding one-time, nonrecurring transactions), and return on investment is 13.8 percent or more (based on total corporate assets as of October 31, less lease-back arrangements concluded in the preceding nine months), and inventory turnover rate exceeds 4.8 for the fiscal year." If Charley and his wife are planning on using bonus money under that plan for a two-week stay in Hawaii to soak up some February sun, they had better reconcile themselves to a tanning salon in the local shopping mall.

The third danger is a bonus plan that is not specific in its qualifications: "Bonus shall be paid in the event significant sales increases are achieved for the year." You read that and ask the boss how the term "significant" is defined. He throws a manly arm across your shoulder and says that an 11-percent increase is the traditional cutoff point but not to worry because he's sure you can do the job. If you accept his oral assurances, you are headed for trouble down the road. The trouble can come in a number of forms. You may have a new boss at the end of the year and his definition of "significant" may be a 20-percent increase. You can have the same boss but he may be under pressure to reduce costs and will have "forgotten" about your conversation and "significant" is now 15 percent. The term "sales" may suddenly be defined as involving net prices when you thought it meant list prices or the costs of shipping goods may be deducted from your sales. There is a host of ways in which a vaguely written bonus plan can be interpreted to your disadvantage.

To protect yourself from "misunderstandings," make sure the goals set for you are specific and quantifiable. This means that all relevant terms should be defined and a number assigned to each goal: "For the year, production of bottle caps shall average no fewer than 150,000 per shift per working day." If a number cannot be assigned, then something tangible should be the outcome of your effort: a computer program that is up and running by a certain date, for example, or a report to be submitted by a specific date. Performance goals that are not based on numbers or tangible results are subject to interpretation. Since it is the company that will be doing the interpreting, the assumption can reasonably be made that the interpretation will be based on the company's best interests, not yours.

It is usually only the goals for middle managers that are set so high that extraordinary accomplishments are necessary to receive the extra pay. Top management seldom demands much of itself. *Fortune* magazine points out that at NCR Corporation bonuses for top executives will be paid only when return on equity exceeds 6 percent. Do not weep for the biggies at NCR, however; 6 percent ROI is five points below the worst return that NCR has had in the past five years. At Sears, bonuses are paid when the company ranks in the seventeenth percentile on ROI among a group of similar companies, Sears couldn't miss that goal if they tried. At Warner-Lambert the rules were changed to exclude losses from divestitures and phased-out product lines; otherwise no one would have received a bonus. Graef S. Crystal, a compensation specialist with Towers Perrin Forster & Crosby, has said, "Most managements have little appetite for establishing really gutty targets." Two exceptions are Wang Labs, where ROI must exceed fifteen percent and other goals must be met to earn a bonus, and H.J. Heinz, where goals include a 7-percent rise in earnings per share and a substantial increase in price per share.

As a footnote to the discussion of performance bonuses,

it is interesting that affirmative-action programs at many corporations were going nowhere until specific quotas for hiring and promoting women and minorities were made part of the goals each manager needed to reach in order to qualify for a year-end bonus. In many companies that was the key that opened doors that had previously been locked tight. That the Civil Rights Act of 1964 specifically forbade the use of numerical quotas was ignored, apparently on the assumption that the end justified the means.

How prevalent are bonuses, what is their range, and which companies pay the most? The Executive Compensation Service of the American Management Association publishes an annual report on executive compensation that can help to answer those questions. The ECS surveyed 1,451 companies about their executive compensation for the calendar year 1981 and found that 61 percent had a bonus or incentive plan of some kind. Bonuses averaged 36.1 percent of base salaries. That last figure is distorted by the lavish bonuses paid to CEOs by many companies; the median would probably be between 15 and 20 percent. The survey showed that in general larger companies paid larger bonuses and there was little correlation between profitability and bonus awards. For middle managers, bonuses ranged between 7 and 24 percent of salary.

It is difficult to determine bonus schedules for individual companies, but a rough guideline is provided by bonuses paid to CEOs. The assumption can be made that if the CEO gets a fat bonus, the largesse is distributed similarly down the line. On that assumption the following information from *Forbes* magazine and *Fortune* magazine might prove helpful to those seeking the big payoff:

Company	CEO	1981 Salary	1981 Bonus
W.R. Grace	J. Peter Grace	$549,000	$1,265,000
Gulf & Western	Charles Bludhorn	870,000	554,000

Company	CEO	*1981 Salary*	*1981 Bonus*
Union Oil of California	Fred Hartley	$531,000	$800,000
Sears	Edward Telling	650,000	350,000
Winn-Dixie	Bert L. Thomas	None	425,000

Two comments need to be made here. Peter Grace's usual bonus is $265,000, but in 1981 his board of directors awarded him a special bonus of $1 million, "in recognition of his accomplishments during his 36-year tenure as the company's chief executive." Apparently the board was referring to the fact that during those thirty-six years Grace stockholders anjoyed an annual compounded return on their investment of 7.4 percent. In that same period the Standard & Poor's composite stock index showed an average annual return of 10.3 percent.

Devotees of cash bonuses must love Winn-Dixie. Executives of that supermarket chain receive no salaries, only bonuses, and, based on the bonus of the CEO, the goals must be somewhat challenging.

Severance Settlements

In past years, managers who faithfully performed their duties could look forward with some assurance to continued employment and, eventually, retirement on a modest pension. Amid the other vagaries of corporate life, managers now have a relatively new problem to face. Companies have become as fickle in their affections as Scarlett O'Hara at a plantation ball. A corporation will shamelessly replace a faithful servant with the first pretty face that catches its eye, falling in and out of love with managers at a rate that would cause Moll Flanders to blush in dismay. Hardly a manager lives who can say of his company as did Keats of his lady, "She is so constant to me and so kind."

Fading corporate romances used to affect mainly middle-aged and middle-level managers who were presumed to have lost their vigor, but the epidemic has now reached the board rooms and executive suites. The precipitous sacking of CEOs has reached such alarming proportions that the *New York Times Magazine* featured the happening in a cover story. The list of yesterday's heroes who have been unceremoniously dumped by their once adoring boards of directors reads like an all-star lineup of corporate executives: Ross M. Hett of Avco, Reuben Gutoff of Standard Brands, John Schneider of CBS, Arthur Taylor of CBS, John Bakke of CBS (do you get the teensiest feeling that William Paley is a bit hard to please?), Tex James of the *New York Daily News,* Edgar Griffiths of RCA, Bill Seawell of Pan Am, Lee Iacocca of Ford, Lyman Hamilton of ITT, Derick Daniels of Playboy, and Archie McCardell of International Harvester. In Great Britain, not even a title ensures against termination: Sotheby Parke Bernet Group Ltd. recently bid adieu to its CEO, the Earl of Westmoreland, after he presided over two years of declining profits. Joining the peer in departure were four senior executives, and the five are now presumably on the dole.

What is a lad to do when at any moment his inamorata is likely to order him from her sight, never to return? The answer, of course, is to acknowledge the transitory nature of corporate romance and protect yourself against the day when the love light in your employer's eye begins to dim—hence, the severance settlement. Fortunately, corporations, unlike the heartless loves of my youth, suffer pangs of conscience when a romance is over, and a severance settlement can often be extracted to ease the company's guilt. At least this is so in the case of a CEO whose affections are no longer reciprocated. It is a flinty-hearted corporation that today would cast off a CEO without a cash settlement to soften the pain of rejection. Frequently, these parting bouquets are so generous that the most commonly heard phrase in a company after the boss has been bounced is, "Give me the same deal and they can fire me tomorrow!"

Alas, severance settlements seldom extend very deeply into the managerial layers of a company. But for those who receive the conscience money of a big corporation, the pay-off can be sweet indeed. When Ross Hett was given a final embrace by Avco, the company pressed $900,000 into his palm, payable over five years, and $35,000 annually after that for the rest of his life. Derick Daniels walked away from Playboy blotting his tears with greenbacks valued at $470,000. (Mr. Daniels fell victim to a new phenomenon in American business; he was replaced by the boss's daughter, age 29.) When the Tribune Company bid adieu to Tex James, he smiled through his tears and accepted a lifetime annual pension of $103,000, in addition to a ten-year consulting contract worth $50,000 a year. Bill Seawell of Pan Am has cause to feel slighted; when the airline decided it was "up, up, and awayyy" with a new CEO, all Bill got was a two-year consultant contract worth a meager 200 G's. How's a guy to feel when his sweetheart dumps him that hard? John Bakke of CBS is reputed to have received more than a million dollars as heart balm from CBS, but the rumor is that the payments are spread out and can be cancelled if Mr. Bakke discusses his departure.

In the Age of Merger and the Era of Leveraged-Buyout, the life expectancy of top managers often seems akin to that of a Mayfly. With corporate raiders like Victor Posner and Carl Icahn riding the range, and acquisition addicts like Charley Bluhdorn and Saul Steinberg ever on the prowl for another "hit," it behooves managers of likely takeover targets to protect themselves. Prudent executive teams are fashioning "golden parachutes" in the event their company is taken over or merged into another.

When Conoco became a takeover prize, the company quickly provided protection from peril for Ralph Bailey, the chairman, and eight other officers. Their "parachutes" were designed to snap open as soon as more than 20 percent of Conoco stock was acquired by someone else. Should thereafter one of the officers leave either through termination or resignation, he would be paid a lump sum equal to his next seven years' compensation, less 9 percent. The day after du Pont acquired its controlling interest in

Conoco, Mr. Bailey could have decided that he could "no longer discharge" his duties and walk away with a check for more than $5 million.

Mr. Bailey stayed, but four top executives at Mohasco Corporation decided to cash in their chips even though Gulf and Western's takeover attempt was thwarted. According to the assistant to the president at Mohasco, the four decided to "head for greener hills" and packed $829,000 in their picnic basket.

When Martin Marietta Corporation found itself being ardently pursued by Bendix Corporation, the company quickly granted long-term salary protection to twenty-nine of its executives and then called upon United Technologies for assistance. United Technologies already had sixty-four of its officers equipped with golden parachutes and promptly made an offer for Bendix. William Agee, CEO of Bendix, appealed to his board for reassurance and the board promptly granted $16 million in salary guarantees to the company's top sixteen officers (Agee's share was $4 million) and called upon Allied Corporation to live up to its name and serve as their ally. Allied leaped into the fray, having already provided its CEO, Edward Hennessey, with a 24-karat parachute worth $3.9 million. None of those ripcords has yet been pulled but the betting is that Agee will be the first to hit the silk.

Brunswick, Control Data, Phillips Petroleum and Superior Oil are among the companies providing "Special Termination Agreements" in the event of a takeover. The number of executives covered ranges from four or five to twenty-five and the payouts for the CEOs start at $870,000 and go up to $5.6 million. Kimberly-Clark Corporation must feel like a homecoming queen at a fraternity toga party; to ward off unwanted suitors, K-C has guaranteed· the salaries of eighty of its executives for far into the future. If all the executives at Beneficial Corporation use their "parachutes," it will look like a NATO airborne landing; 234 of Beneficial's executives are covered, which must include everyone down to the mailroom supervisor. So far, no payments have been made at these companies, but those involved sleep better each night.

For mergers of a less salubrious nature, casualties are to be expected. Usually, protection is given only to the half dozen or so top executives, but AMF has agreements covering every corporate vice president, twenty-five in all, for a period of ten years. Often the pacts provide benefits for resignations as well as involuntary terminations. Sunbeam will allow its senior executives to quit within ninety days of a takeover and take home six months severance pay. Brunswick Corporation allows directors more than fifty-five years old to retire after a takeover and receive $22,000 annually for life. Control Data will allow its officers to resign after a takeover and get paid at three times the normal rate for the length of their contracts.

Some severance agreements pay off only upon termination, not resignation, but afford protection against the tactic of forced resignation ("Charley, I know you're a vice president at $150,000 a year, but from now on your office is in the men's toilet"). The severance agreement is made effective if the executive's duties or working conditions are substantially changed. AMF protects its people from a common tactic used on unwanted executives, unceasing travel. If an AMF manager is on the road for more than twenty-one consecutive days or one hundred days in a year, he can leave and receive his severance settlement. When McLean Trucking was merged into the Meridian Company, the executives at McLean received an agreement that none would be relocated for five years.

Terminations are not caused solely by mergers and acquisitions. We have all been in, or seen, situations where a new company president or even a new department head has meant a wholesale replacement of the staff. People are terminated for a variety of reasons: The new boss wants his own people, who will be loyal to him and not to the old administration. Changes are made that the old staff has difficulty in accepting and the new boss gets impatient and gets rid of the holdovers. Terminations are made by the new boss to demonstrate his authority or because the president made it a condition of the job. The old boss was ineffective and the staff became tarred by the same brush, thereby becoming candidates for departure. The new boss has a style that is incompatible with the staff and forces resignations. Profits are down and the board feels a shakeup is necessary, so a new team is brought in. Whatever the reason, corporate managers know they live with the possibility of imminent termination. Effectiveness in your job offers some protection but it is not absolute. Your best course is to accept the reality of corporate life and take what action prudence dictates. One cushion you should try to provide yourself is a severance settlement.

As with any other perk, the best time to negotiate a severance agreement is before you accept a new position. If you present the request as a natural reaction to the uncertainties of business life, it should not be resented. You are not asking for a severance agreement because you have doubts about your ability to do the job; you are simply seeking some prudent protection against an unforeseen but fairly common occurrence in business. Companies are acquired, bought, sold, merged, and spun off. Even without those changes, a company can change its management style, its CEO, its lines of business or its marketing thrust. When the Mary Carter Paint Company became Resorts International and stopped selling paint to get into the casino gambling business, how many of its managers found their skills transferable? When Penn Central got out of the railroad business and into real estate and mining, did all those old railroad hands smoothly switch over? When Singer got out of computers and a batch of other businesses unrelated to sewing machines, how many managers found themselves on the pavement? If companies are entitled to shift direction or leadership without warning, then managers are entitled to protection against those changes.

If you don't have a severance agreement, what can you do when the boss calls you in and says it's a new ball game and they have to let you go to make room on the team for a newcomer? First, don't panic. If it's your first firing, you'll think it's the end of the world. It isn't and, in more cases than not, it's probably a good thing. If you haven't been fired before, you've probably been with your company too long and gotten complacent. Now is your chance to evaluate your career and decide what you want to do, where you want to do it and who you want to do it with. If you treat the firing as an opportunity, that is what it will become and you will end up with a better job at more pay; any executive recruiter can tell you a hundred stories of exactly that happening.

The most important aspect of your recovery is to understand that once again you are in a negotiating situation. You do not have to take your accrued vacation pay and quietly slip away. You can protect yourself by negotiating for cash and other benefits that will make a significant difference in your ability to rebound from this temporary setback. Remember, the company is hoping you will silently fold your tent and be seen no more so your presence will not be a reminder of their guilt. This is not the time to be the good scout you've always been. It is now time to begin looking out for Number One. You no longer need be concerned about pleasing your boss or not making waves within the company. Don't worry about a negative reference your company might give to a prospective employer. Companies are so afraid of lawsuits that no one gives negative references any more.

If the company is the least bit hesitant about acceding to your severance settlement demands, use the power of the law to bring it to heel. If you are over forty, mention that your attorney brother-in-law is urging you to file an age-discrimination suit. If you are a woman, threaten sexual discrimination or sexual harassment. If your heritage is anything other than northern European, threaten racial or ethnic discrimination. If you are Catholic, Jewish, Hindu, Moslem, or anything other than Protestant, threaten religious bias. If you are homosexual, overweight, or handicapped in any way, the courts will be happy to entertain your suit for discrimination. And if you really want to make the company sweat, threaten a class action suit on behalf of all employees like you who were dismissed in the past ten years. When the company contemplates the possibility of punitive triple damages should a class action suit prove successful, it will become surprisingly accommodating. Let the company know that you're not hostile, just aggrieved and hurt by its action. You aren't certain what to do, but if the company will make your departure a bit less traumatic, it probably won't be necessary to appeal to the courts for assistance. You want to be reasonable and you are sure the company does also.

With the proper combination of carrot and stick, the company will become very reasonable. First, you want to negotiate the largest cash settlement you can. Forget about company guidelines that say you are only entitled to one week's severance pay for each year of employment. You are entitled to all you can get. Haggle, bargain, negotiate. If you are insistent, it is virtually certain you can do better than the sum allotted under company policy.

If company policy is absolutely rigid on severance pay, then get the company to keep you on the payroll longer; the effect is the same. If you would have been entitled to a year-end bonus or sales commissions, demand all or part of the money you would have received. If you would have been vested in a larger portion of your profit-sharing or pension plan in a few months, demand that your employment records be adjusted to provide that.

Second, you will need a base of operations while you are job hunting. Get the company to assign you an office where you can make phone calls, have letters typed and résumés reproduced, take incoming calls, and mail out correspondence. It's always easier to get a job when you have one rather than when you need one; there's no reason for prospective employers to know that once a week you are making new friends in the line at the unemployment office. A company-provided office maintains the illusion of employment.

Third, push hard for the use of an out-placement service, company-paid, of course. Aside from helping with your résumé and job search, a good out-placement counsellor provides much needed psychic assistance. Being out of work is an extremely trying, emotional time, especially for those of us who define ourselves by what we do. The cost of an out-placement service will probably be 10 to 15 percent of your previous annual salary, but don't let that deter you. Ask for it. You need it, and the company owes it to you.

Other things you can ask for are continued use of the company car until you find another job, medical and dental coverage until you are safe within the benefit programs of another company, a travel allowance to help defray job-hunting costs, and, if applicable, the costs of relocation back to your previous town.

Remember, he who will not ask, will not receive.

Freelance Work

Are you talented? Do you have a skill other people are willing to pay for? Can you sell your services? If so, you could be making money over and above the salary your company pays you. Some companies are very touchy about outside work being done by their employees. Some couldn't care less, while others simply ignore a situation they know exists. If you are earning outside income now with the knowledge of your company, you are in a fortunate position. Most moonlighters have to do it on the sly. If you are forced to tend your still in the woods behind everyone's back, perhaps it is time you came to an understanding with your company that will allow you to continue your activities without fear of censure if discovered. Or, if you are about to take a new job and expect to do outside work, you should have a clear agreement as to the nature and extent of your extra-mural activities.

Perhaps you've never thought about outside work, figuring that it is done on weekends by painters or carpenters. Much of moonlit work is done by skilled tradesmen, but even more is done by people in a hundred other occupations. Recent studies place the extent of the "underground economy" at 10 to 15 percent of the gross national product. The attraction for many is that income often need not appear on a tax return. Either payment is made in cash that goes unreported or the work is bartered for a needed service. Many corporate accountants do the books of their doctors or dentists in return for free medical or dental work. Corporate lawyers regularly prepare wills and handle real estate transactions for friends and tradesmen who reciprocate with goods or services.

The extent of the so-called underground economy is impossible to determine, but even conservative estimates put it in the billions of dollars each year. The claim has even been made that if all moonlight dollars were taxed, the federal budget could be balanced. Those holding that belief underestimate the spending abilities of politicians, but there is no question that moonlighting is a way of life for millions of Americans.

What opportunities for freelance work are available to corporate managers? Herewith, a partial list:

1. Private practice by lawyers and accountants
2. Professional work by photographers, designers, and artists
3. Publishing assignments for writers and editors
4. Programming jobs for computer specialists
5. Teaching of evening business courses by seasoned, articulate managers
6. Consulting assignments for engineers
7. Conducting public seminars by training managers
8. Owning a small business

The list is not complete because the imagination of those in pursuit of money is all but unlimited, but it might serve to spark an idea for those of you whose time has come. If you do get involved in moonlighting, it is best that your boss know about it. You and he should look upon it as a perk accompanying the special skills you bring to your regular job.

— 5 —

Relocation Expenses

In the 1960s those of us who worked at IBM were certain the company initials stood for "I've Been Moved." In those days, if you were an upwardly mobile manager at IBM, or almost any Fortune 500 company, you could expect to be promoted every three years or so, with relocation accompanying almost every promotion. Things have settled down since then, and companies no longer relocate their employees unless there is no way of avoiding it. I would like to think that wholesale relocations have been reduced because companies came to an awareness of the trauma inflicted upon spouses and children; the reality is that lower profits in the 1970s and escalating moving costs have forced the change.

Homequity Inc., a large relocation service, reports that it now costs an average of $40,000 to move a family of four 1,000 miles. That is four times the cost of a similar move in 1976. That cost does not include the additional expenses the company might incur in providing mortgage assistance to the transferred employee or in buying the employee's previous residence, which could not be sold in today's real estate market. Looking at those costs, most companies have decided that it usually isn't absolutely necessary to send Charley out to the plant in Danville for a couple of years of seasoning before bringing him back to the home office. At the same time, if Charley does go to the plant in Danville, he can figure on spending quite a few years there while he works his way up to plant manager. Unless he then outhustles the other plant managers and becomes vice president of manufacturing, it is unlikely that Charley will ever be moved back to corporate headquarters.

Managers now have to think much more carefully about accepting a promotion that involves relocation. No longer can you do so with the knowledge that once you have performed well you can depend upon a return to headquarters with another promotion. You have to consider the distinct possibility that you may spend the rest of your career in Danville. Few managers today will accept relocation unless it is part of a significant promotion, rather than one more small step among many on the career ladder; the move should represent a quantum leap in income, opportunity, and responsibility. To separate yourself from corporate headquarters, perhaps permanently, is not worth it, if you get anything less.

Even then, many companies are finding it difficult to persuade managers to uproot themselves and their families. This is especially true if the move is to Detroit, Cleveland, Boston, Chicago, or any Frost Belt city where living costs are high and the quality of life appears to be less than it is back home. Conversely, managers who have learned to appreciate the challenge and stimulation of those cities will resist moves to smaller cities in the Sun Belt where many companies are opening new plants or offices. New York and California are special cases. Almost no one wants to move away from the starlets on Hollywood Boulevard to the muggers on 42nd Street. In the other direction, many a hopeful transferee has slunk back to Madison Avenue after vainly looking for a house or condominium he could afford in sometimes sunny California.

When companies feel it is essential to transfer an employee they now offer a basketfull of goodies to make the move more palatable. If you are asked to relocate, make sure the career opportunity and increase in income justify the move. Once that decision is made, make sure you get all of what's available in terms of relocation expenses.

When you discover the hidden costs of moving and what the movers do to your furniture, all that you can get won't be enough.

House-hunting Costs

A minimum of three visits by you and your spouse to the new location will be needed in order to find a suitable residence. Choosing a home in which you are going to live and raise a family is not a task to be done carelessly or in haste. Take your time, get to know the community, talk to realtors, residents, co-workers and anyone else who can give you insight into the new city, its neighborhoods, and its problems. Before you visit the city write to the Chamber of Commerce and ask for maps, historical data, and information on schools, churches, transportation, recreational facilities, and anything else that might prove helpful. Have your company office there send you copies of the local newspaper so you can get a feel for the area and the concerns of the people who live there. The more you know about your new location before you start your search for a home or apartment, the better you will be able to evaluate the desirability of what the realtors show you.

All house-hunting costs for you and your wife should be fully reimbursed by the company. That includes air fares, rental cars, hotels, meals, and entertainment while you are relaxing in the evening from the rigors of house hunting. If you must hire a babysitter while you are away, that cost should also be covered. Don't forget that once you have decided upon a home, you will have to return at least once for the closing.

If your company has a written policy on relocation expenses, get a copy before your first trip and study it carefully. Do not feel bound by its restrictions. If it only provides for two house-hunting trips, negotiate for at least one more on an if-needed basis. Examine the policy statement thoroughly and make sure that it provides full coverage for all the expenses you anticipate. If you foresee a problem area, negotiate adjustments before leaving on your initial visit to the new location; do not wait until you are in difficulty before seeking relief.

Temporary Living Costs

It is not always possible to coordinate exactly the moving out and moving in of two parties. Often, people must sell their old residence and move to a new city before the new residence is available. Sometimes this occurs because the company is eager to get the manager in place as quickly as possible; more often it is because the chain of moves cannot be timed perfectly. Regardless of the reason, the company is obligated to pay living expenses for you and your family until the new residence is available. The temporary living costs include motel accommodations for you and your family. You may be in temporary quarters for a number of weeks, so make sure that your rooms are spacious enough to provide a reasonably comfortable existence. If you and your wife are forced to spend extra time settling disputes among children who are feeling the effects of close quarters, you are not going to be able to perform well in your work.

All meal expenses for you and your family should be covered. You will not earn extra credit for feeding your family off a hot plate in your motel room. Eat in decent restaurants and if you want to hold costs down, order the house wine instead of your usual Lafite Rothschild '76. Laundry costs should also be covered, as well as the expense of renting an automobile if yours is in storage or transit. The company should also pay for the cost of storing your household possessions while you are waiting for your new home to become available.

If company policy places a time limit or total dollar limit on your temporary living expenses, make sure the limits are more than adequate to cover your needs. If not, a negotiated adjustment prior to the move will avoid considerable unhappiness later.

The IRS places a limit of $1,500 on deductions for house-hunting and temporary living costs combined. Don't allow your company relocation manager to intimidate you with this sum. All it means is that the company cannot claim more than $1,500 as a business expense. The usual procedure is to have costs in excess of $1,500 added to your pay as a bonus, with an additional amount provided to cover the income taxes you will pay on the "bonus."

Direct Moving Expenses

Do not be misled by the moving company name in the Yellow Pages or the sign on the van; you are not being moved by Bekins Van Lines or Allied or Mayflower or any other nationwide moving service. You will be moved by the local agent who represents the big company. The service you get will be determined by the management of the local agent and the type of people working for him. The national van line companies make an effort to insure that their local agents provide proper service, but it is impossible for them to completely monitor the behavior of the thousands of agents they deal with. Before contracting with a mover, get the names of three or four recent customers and find out what sort of service was provided. It isn't enough that goods were moved from one place to another. Were the goods picked up and delivered when specified? Was the work done courteously, carefully, and efficiently? How much damage was done? How did the insurance company for the mover handle the insurance claim? The answers to these and other questions will help you make an informed decision on which moving company to select. The Interstate Commerce Commission will provide you with a copy of the latest performance report on any carrier you are considering. Write to: Interstate Commerce Commission, 12th and Constitution Avenues, N.W., Washington, D.C. 20423.

The agreement with the movers should include packing all possessions at the old location and unpacking them at the new. All transportations costs for the family, including pets, should be provided for by your company. You should receive a mileage allowance for the movement of your automobile; it is a business expense just as if you used it to call on a customer. If your car or cars need to be driven by a third party, the expense of that service should also be paid by the company. The IRS does not allow the company to deduct the cost of moving your boat, so a "bonus" may need to be agreed upon. If you use a relocation service, the company should pay that fee. The IRS does not set any dollar limit on deductions for direct moving costs, so you needn't concern yourself about staying under a certain figure.

Your company should provide full insurance coverage for your possessions while they are in transit or in storage. The company coverage is necessary because the moving company only provides insurance of 60¢ per pound for damage or loss. This means that if the movers lose a box full of bricks you might break even, but on anything else you'll lose money. The moving company will make extra insurance protection available to you at additional cost, which should be passed on to your company. It is also helpful to have protection from your company's insurance in case of catastrophe. Some years ago a friend of mine was transferred from Los Angeles to Chicago. He and his family drove to Chicago in the family station wagon and were there informed that the van containing all the possessions from their eight-room house had been destroyed by fire while in transit. If IBM had not provided additional insurance their out-of-pocket loss would have amounted to almost $20,000.

Indirect Expenses

You are probably going to have to sell your house quickly in order to take over your new job as soon as the company would like. This means you must hire a realtor in order to find potential buyers, thereby incurring a realtor's fee of 6 or 7 percent. On a less than lavish house these days the realtor's fee could amount to $10,000 or more. If the move were being made on your own initiative, you could take your time and find your own buyers, thereby saving the realtor's fee. It is only equitable that the company pay the realtor's fee.

The attorney who handles the sale of your old house and his counterpart who handles the purchase of the new home will each charge a fee. Those fees should be paid by the company.

There is an IRS limit of $3,000 on deductible *indirect* moving costs, which includes the $1,500 limit on expenses for house-hunting and temporary living costs. Any excess should be added to your income with a "kicker" to cover the additional income taxes.

Mortgage Differential

Marcus Aurelius said that "very little is needed to make a happy life," and today that very little is often a 7.5 percent mortgage. Are you the possessor of a mortgage obtained before our political leaders decided that if a little inflation is good a lot of inflation is better? If so, you should be a happy person indeed. Some of us can remember the post-war years when homes were bought with no money down and a 4½ percent mortgage. Those modest houses in Levittown or Shady Acres bought for $8,000 now sell for $70,000 or more and the mortgage rate is close to 13 percent.

So here you are—a happy individual—and the company offers a promotion that appeals to you. You accept the promotion and begin your house search in the new city. You quickly find that the inflated value of your old house, which seemed so thrilling when you contemplated it, now provides nothing more than a down payment on a new house. If you are lucky, the new home will be equal to the old; if you are moving from a small town to a city, or from anywhere to California, your new home will probably cost more and be smaller and in a less desirable neighborhood than the one you had before.

But most distressing is the realization that your mortgage costs may very well double. On a $75,000 mortgage at 7½ percent, the first month's interest is $468.75. A comparable mortgage at 13 percent would have a first month's interest charge of $812.50. The ratio of difference will remain the same for the life of the mortgage although the dollar difference will change as the principal is paid down. You may console yourself with the knowledge that you will have a massive deduction off your income tax for interest paid out, but the reality is that you will be incurring thousands of dollars of extra housing costs each year and for many, many years into the future. You should not bear that burden alone.

Many companies now pay the difference in mortgage rates for an employee going from a low-interest mortgage to a higher one. Initially, most companies agreed to pay the differential for no more than three years, reasoning that by then mortgage rates would have descended from the stratosphere and assistance would no longer be required. Companies are now reevaluating that policy and in many cases are making commitments for four or five years. Ideally, you should have a sliding scale of payments that continue until your new mortgage can be refinanced at the same rate as the old.

Whether your company provides assistance with the mortgage differential or not, you should not agree to a mortgage in which there is a penalty for paying it off early.

Housing Subsidy

Aside from the increased cost of a higher mortgage rate, in many transfers a manager is faced with higher prices for homes or apartments. A few years ago, a friend of mine was transferred from his company's headquarters in New York to a subsidiary in Los Angeles. He found a buyer for his four-bedroom colonial home in northern New Jersey. The selling price was close to $80,000 and represented a handsome appreciation over its original cost. My friend and his wife left for a house-hunting trip to southern California, knowing they would have $60,000 to use as a down payment on a new house. They felt it was time to move up in their living style and decided to look for houses selling for around $125,000. Three days later, after visiting a number of realtors and seeing many homes in their anticipated price range, the wife had to be sedated. In southern California, $125,000 would buy them a small bungalow in a depressing neighborhood, and usually the house was a "fixer-upper." They finally settled for a much smaller house than they had in the East, in arid land 40 miles from Los Angeles. The house was on a small plot in a new development with no trees or greenery and cost $160,000 but, this being Southern California, it did have a small backyard pool. By accepting the transfer, my friend found his standard of living significantly reduced because of the difference in housing costs, a factor over which he had no control.

Another friend was also transferred from New York to Los Angeles but, learning from the experiences of others, negotiated a five-year housing subsidy of $600 per month. This was over and above all other reimbursements for relocation and special provisions such as three years of mortgage assistance. The housing subsidy has become an accepted part of executive transfers. Some companies have even developed mathematical formulas so that negotiations are not necessary; you tell the company where you are moving from and your new home town and they run the formula to determine your subsidy. Before accepting any transfer you should determine the difference in housing costs between the two locations. If the difference is significant, a housing subsidy is in order for at least three years.

Settling-in Allowance

Many companies provide funds for the miscellaneous expenses inevitably incurred during a move that are difficult to itemize. The allowance is sometimes referred to as "curtain money" or "carpet money," derived from the extra expense of refitting carpets and drapes. The payment is not just for those items but for all the minor expenses of moving that when added together can amount to a substantial sum. The usual settling-in allowance is one month's salary.

If that seems rather generous for small expenses, consider the unreimburseable damages to your furniture. Before the movers touch anything, they note all marks, dents, knicks, scratches, and imperfections. A table that then has a leg knocked off in moving is considered to be of little value because the mover had noted a scratch on top and a nick on the side. On paper, the notations make it seem you only buy furniture from Salvation Army outlets and then call in the neighborhood children to savage it. In reality the scratch and nick on the table might have been barely visible, but you will have a tough time winning that argument with the insurance company. If you have antiques or other items of real value, protect yourself with close-up photographs from all sides.

The settling-in allowance will offer some compensation for an aspect of relocation my wife and I discovered some years ago: After three moves you need all new furniture.

Unusual Costs

Each move is different and company policy must be adjusted accordingly. The *New York Times* tells of one executive transferred by his company who was also a gentleman farmer. To make the move, the company had to agree to transport the executive's herd of pregnant sheep across the country. Another executive had a child with a hearing problem that was being well compensated in a special class in the local public school district. The schools in the new location had no such program and the company therefore paid for a private school. Apartment dwellers should have the costs of an apartment-location service paid, as well as the fee charged by the real estate broker who manages the apartment they eventually choose.

When Robert Hunt was sent to New York by the Tribune Company to run the *Daily News,* he was given a

$495,000 interest-free loan for leaving the balmy climes of Chicago. Pan Am made things simple for Charles Acker when he took over as CEO: The company found and purchased a suitable Manhattan apartment. In New York City, that is considered the ultimate Perk! CBS should have done the same for the chief financial officer they brought in from San Francisco. After six months of fruitless apartment hunting he quit to return to California. When an executive earning more than $200,000 a year cannot find a suitable apartment in Manhattan, you can imagine what the rest of us are living in! If your company is transferring you to Manhattan, get some financial protection or don't make the move.

— 6 —

Peace of Mind

Serenity of mind and calmness of thought are a better enjoyment.

Benjamin Whichcote

Periodically the Western world rediscovers the attractions of the Orient. The fall of Rome and Byzantium produced a hiatus in our contacts with the East, but Marco Polo resumed the process in the thirteenth century when he returned to Venice with wondrous tales of Cathay and its perplexing society. It soon became the rage in Europe to own garments of silk or to serve that strange new beverage, tea. When Commodore Perry opened Japan to foreign trade it wasn't long before no lawn party in America was complete without Japanese lanterns. Soon Gilbert and Sullivan wrote *The Mikado* and kicked off a craze in England for all things Japanese. James Hilton's novel *Lost Horizon* fostered the belief that the Orient contains a wisdom and serenity unknown in the pushy, materialistic West. During the 1960s the Beatles led hordes of youthful wanderers to India, seeking the meaning of life. And in the late Seventies we had gaggles of American executives and business school professors returning from Japan with exotic tales of the secrets of Japanese management that allowed them to excel in the battle for world markets.

How much of Japan's success is due to consensus-style management skills and how much to other factors is not known, but the following story may be instructive. Some years ago a friend of mine was in Japan on a consulting assignment and visited an electronics factory. He noticed that the workers assembling components at their benches were all wearing black armbands. He asked the company guide if the company president had died. The guide replied, "Oh, no, the workers are on strike and wear the armbands to show their unhappiness; of course, they then work much harder to show their company loyalty." It may be argued that Japanese-style management produces that kind of intense company devotion, but I think the answer goes deeper into Japanese culture and tradition.

One of the much-extolled virtues of Japan, Inc., is the system of lifetime employment offered by the larger Japanese corporations. Supposedly, this feature of Japanese business life enables their executives to focus on the long-term best interests of their company and not worry about today's Profit & Loss Statement.

American executives have no such security, and the saying in the board rooms is that you're only as good as the prior quarter results. How much of all this is true is problematical, but it is certain that American firms are much quicker to jettison a manager on a temporary losing streak than companies in Japan or even Europe. It would seem then that an American manager who can attain a modicum of inner serenity has an advantage in the unending competition for jobs, promotions, and market share. The trick, of course, is to remain serene while competing zestfully in the struggle for personal advancement.

Business life is not for those whose security needs have first priority; for them, the traditional safe harbors of government, education, and church are the preferred anchorages. Yet even for those in business whose first priorities are accomplishment and advancement, it is only prudent to fashion whatever security is possible. Herewith are some of the means by which executives seek to insulate themselves from the icy winds of fate.

A No-Cut Contract

Blessings upon him who first devised the no-cut contract. Perhaps it was Pope Sylvester I who persuaded the Council of Nicaea in 325 A.D., and, more importantly, the Emperor Constantine to give him and all his successors lifetime, non-cancellable contracts. James M. Kerr of Avco didn't do so badly in this area, either. Kerr's contract provided for a salary of $310,000 a year until retirement, at which time he was to receive approximately $500,000 paid out over fifteen years, all this in addition to a pension commensurate with his status. Kerr was succeeded by Robert P. Bauman, who accepted a five-year, no-cut contract paying $300,000 annually, in addition to bonuses. Stanton Cook of the Tribune Company is guaranteed $300,000 a year until 1990, in addition to other goodies. (Three-hundred thousand dollars seems a popular figure in no-cut contracts these days.) Of course, few executive contracts can compare with those of top baseball or hockey stars, but entertainment has always been more rewarding than honest enterprise.

Assuming you're not a CEO negotiating for the usual $300,000 a year, is it possible to obtain a no-cut contract for yourself? It is, but once again you'll probably have to change companies and go with someone who really wants you; you make the no-cut contract part of your package of perks. The terms of no-cut contracts are usually fairly simple: the company agrees to pay you so much for so many years, no matter what. Often, the only out for a company is if you are convicted of a felony offense and cannot adequately perform your duties from a prison cell. Mental or physical incapacity should not invalidate the agreement. After all, if Dave Winfield's batting eye goes bad, George Steinbrenner still has to pay him a million dollars a year for 15 years.

An interesting provision of some contracts is that the company must arrange a new agreement no later than twelve months before the old one expires. If a new contract is not signed at that time, the executive is free to spend the next year seeking other employment. In effect, this provision gives you one year's advance notice that your services will no longer be required; you thereby avoid the inconvenience caused by a pink slip and a check for two weeks severance pay.

Pension Benefits

You and the company need not be bound by the terms of the company pension plan. Is that a surprise? It shouldn't be. CEOs are always arranging special pension plans; there is no reason why it can't be done at lower levels except that few ask for it. Does the company plan say you are not eligible until after one year's employment? In all likelihood there was an exception to that rule made in the past, probably when a CEO was hired, and you can qualify under the same exception if the company wants you badly enough. If there is no way around the qualifying period, compute the lost benefit and have the company pay the amount into your IRA account. That way your pension benefits do not suffer because of a job change.

Once you qualify, the amount you and the company place into the company pension plan is set by the terms of the plan, but there is nothing to prevent the company from supplementing the regular pension program. Note that the tax act of 1982 places a maximum annual payout of $90,000 on a company pension to any one individual. In addition to the regular pension program, the company can, for instance, pay all or part of the $2,000 each year you are allowed to put into an IRA account. The payment by the company is reported as taxable income but is offset by the IRA deduction. The advantage is that the IRA is wholly yours; you do not have to wait to become vested in it as is required by many company pension or profit-sharing plans.

The company can also agree to establish a supplementary pension plan for you that can be structured so that money placed into it is not taxed until withdrawn. There are no limits to such supplementary deposits so long as your total pension does not exceed $90,000; it is simply a matter for negotiation.

You should also work out a procedure whereby any funds assigned to you under the regular pension plan can be rolled over into an annuity or otherwise set aside for you should you leave the company. Again, this can be done in a way that does not impose an immediate tax burden.

The reality of company pension plans is that they are actuarily computed on the assumption that, through employee turnover, only a few employees will actually draw money from them. However, there is no need for you to accept that situation. With proper negotiation you can obtain the benefits of corporate pension programs even though you change employers on a regular basis.

Life Insurance

The amount of life insurance provided you by your company is, once again, a matter for negotiation. The American Management Association publishes an annual "Report on Executive Perquisites"; of the 731 companies responding to the 1981 survey, 47 percent provided additional life insurance to their executives. The amounts ranged from $10,000 to $1.5 million, depending upon job level. The additional coverage was usually based on a multiple of the executive's annual income, ranging from one times salary to four times. (This is a method whereby those who have more get more, without subjecting the company to IRS displeasure for discrimination.) There is an IRS rule that should be considered in working out your insurance coverage: You are only allowed $50,000 of company-paid life insurance without penalty. All premiums on life insurance above $50,000 must be reported by your company on your W-2 forms as ordinary income. If you want more than $50,000 of coverage, see if you can get your company to "gross up" your income to cover the additional income tax you will have to pay on the cost of premiums above $50,000.

A different strategy is to hold your life insurance coverage at $50,000 and add substantially to your accidental death and disability coverage. If you are in normal health and under forty-five years of age, the chances of your dying or becoming disabled in an accident are much greater than the chance you will die of an illness. The IRS places no limit on accidental death coverage, and $500,000 worth of protection would seem barely adequate these days for an executive who flies frequently and must go out at night in places like Detroit or Dallas or New York City. If some evening you find yourself in a bar in San Francisco whose patrons are all in leather and chains and one of whom is holding a gun to your ear, you should at least be comforted by the knowledge that your loved ones will be well taken care of by your accidental death policy.

The AMA study shows that 63 percent of the companies provided some sort of special accident insurance for employees while traveling on business. The usual coverage paid $100,000 to $300,000 for accidental death, with lesser amounts for permanent disability or dismemberment.

Paid-up Annuity

A paid-up annuity is like a signing bonus except that you get the money later rather than now. Instead of putting cash in your pocket, it provides ease of mind in knowing that in case of emergency or, more likely, retirement, cash is available when needed. You may not require immediate income (heaven only knows why), but there is no need to forgo the benefit of a signing bonus. The paid-up annuity is the answer. Companies also like annuities because they do not require as much immediate cash outlay as a signing bonus. Annuities increase in value the longer they remain unredeemed, and it is to your advantage to hold on to them as long as possible.

Health Club Membership

> O Health! Health!
> The blessing of the rich!
> The riches of the poor.
> Ben Jonson

Are you under stress? Is your blood pressure too high? Do you smoke too much? Drink more than you should? Is your diet a running joke among nutritionists? Is combing your hair the only exercise you get? Do pills put you to sleep, wake you up, and calm you down? Does the amount of coffee you consume have your doctor muttering about renal failure? Does that lean body of yesteryear look like a Christmas stocking after Santa Claus has stuffed it? Does getting up to turn on the television set cause you to wheeze heavily? Does waving for a taxi cause the muscles in your arm to ache? In short, are you a typical corporate executive?

If so, welcome to the Indolence Club; there are millions of us who are members and, if it's any consolation, most are in worse shape than you. See Wally over there; his doctor just told him that if he doesn't bring his blood pressure down, he won't be here in ten years. Wally's no dummy. He went with another company that provides him with a million-dollar insurance policy and unlimited disability benefits. His blood pressure's the same but when he goes, it will be with a smile.

If you are serious about playing the Perks Game then you must give due consideration to perks involving health and education. It's not enough to be wealthy. To live fully one must also be healthy and wise. Let's start with health. Aside from your own efforts to maintain the proper working of your body, the perks provided by your company can be of great assistance. Health club memberships are now provided by many companies to managers whose fitness is thought important. The cost of a club membership is thought a small price to pay for the reduced absenteeism and increased vigor of the managers involved.

Depending upon the level of opulence, a health club membership can range from $50 a year at the local YMCA to thousands of dollars at spas such as The Vertical Club in New York or La Costa southeast of Los Angeles. Somewhere in between lies a club for you that your company may well agree to pay for. Offer it as a suggestion at your next salary review and it may receive a favorable response. If the company won't pay for the membership as an outright perk, perhaps they will do so and then reduce your next pay increase by the necessary amount. That way you are not paying for your membership with after-tax dollars.

Do you want to obtain the full benefit, including image, of your dynamic and vigorous lifestyle? If so, then your exercising should be done at lunchtime and in such a manner that everyone knows you are pursuing Juvenal's ideal of a sound mind in a healthy body. If you exercise in the morning or evening, who's to know it except those sweating alongside you? (Unless, of course, it's the company president whose exercise schedule you have made your own.)

How to let others know? Invite guests along to share your grunting and straining. Even if you have to pay for their guest fees, it will be worth it if you choose your invitees carefully. Carry a gym bag or squash racquet as you exit the office. Leave the phone number of the club with your secretary so she can let callers know that you can be reached there. Take the last five minutes to lie under the sun lamp; there's nothing like a winter tan to attest to one's devotion to a life of fitness.

Health club membership is a perk that is coming into its own. Sixty-one percent of the companies in the AMA study pay for memberships in country clubs or health clubs. More than half the companies pay only if they can specify the club. Some have a dollar limit on the amount they will pay; those limits average $1,655. (Three companies report no limit on the amount they will pay but, alas, those three names are confidential.) Some companies have gone so far as to build their own exercise facilities. Gould Corporation, northwest of Chicago, has a health club that can stand comparison with any in the country. It has exercise rooms, handball courts, a basketball court, a large pool, sauna and steam rooms, and a running track. Millions were spent on its construction and equipment, and it is available at nominal cost to all Gould employees. The club is an outgrowth of the intense interest that the company president William Ylvisaker has in physical fitness. He contends that the club pays for itself by cutting down on time lost because of illness, by reduced payments for health and life insurance, and through greater productivity from workers who are healthier and more energetic.

A number of other companies have their own health clubs, and most are enthusiastic about the use and positive effects of them. Many office buildings are now being constructed with health clubs built into their design. The clubs are available to tenants of the buildings for an annual fee and add greatly to the appeal of the buildings to companies seeking office space.

Are there dangers in taking time in the middle of the day to exercise? Aside from an occasional sprained ankle or pulled muscle, the greatest danger is spending too much time at the club. A game of squash or racquetball followed by a swim, a session in the sauna, a visit to the sun room, and a shower can easily occupy the better part of two hours before you get back to your office. If two-hour lunches are the norm at your company, there is no problem. If, however, everyone is expected to take no more than sixty minutes at midday, you had better schedule your time at the club accordingly.

Health clubs, if they include tennis or handball courts, can often be a way of meeting others in your company whom you might otherwise not get to know. This is an opportunity to meet your superiors and become friendly with your peers. However, before leaping into the social world of the health club do a little looking. Who are the other members from your company? Is it just your peers, or are top executives there also? What activities do they engage in? What type of socializing goes on? Do employees from all levels mingle freely or do they separate into groups by rank? Do they talk shop? If so, when, under what circumstances, and who initiates the discussion? Does one part of the locker room seem reserved for top management?

Almost every company has one sport that is preeminent—usually whatever the president plays. If possible, become proficient in the preferred sport; you can be assured that the upper-level managers are skilled at it. You may have to spend some weeks or months practicing in the evening before you consider yourself on a par with the better players in the company but it will be time well spent. Take you time, don't be pushy, and soon you will be offered the chance to play with people in the company who outrank you. If you acquit yourself properly, you may someday find yourself playing the president. If so, those hours you spent practicing will have done more for your career than anything you did in the office. (Assuming you give the boss a good game and lose by only a point or two.)

A note of caution. When at the club and in the presence of your superiors, do not initiate shop talk. They are there for relaxation and enjoyment, not to hear your views on reorganizing the credit and collection department. If a higher-level manager does introduce a discussion of company matters, do not join in unless your opinion is specifically asked for, and then state it as concisely as possible.

Annual Physical Exam

What other perks are available to keep you healthy? A company-paid annual physical checkup has become popular. Again, the value of this perk can range from a visit to your family doctor to three days at the Greenbrier Hotel in White Sulphur Springs, West Virginia, where more than one company sends its management team every year. Clinics have sprung up in cities all across the land to provide this service to companies. They are usually owned and staffed by physicians and operate under such names as The Cardio-Fitness Center, The Life Extension Institute, Executive Health Examiners, or Corporate Health Administrative Services.

An annual physical checkup can be a useful perk, but only if the information obtained is reliable and readily available to you. The tests should be conducted by competent laboratories and, in case of doubt, the interpretation of results should be verified by a second opinion. You should receive copies of all the test results or a detailed summary of them. The physician's findings should be in writing, with sufficient detail so that another doctor can draw a clear picture of your physical state at the time of the checkup. All of this documentation provides you with baseline data against which future changes can be measured. In this way, for example, if at some point later on you develop chest pains and the attending doctor runs an EKG, he can have the previous EKG results for comparison. His interpretation of your present condition will then be much more accurate and reliable.

You should also receive recommendations on how to maintain or improve your present physical condition. The recommendations should be specific in suggestions for changes in your diet and physical activity. If a medical problem is discovered, it should be described in detail, with directions on what to do next in terms of further tests or seeing a medical specialist.

Of the companies surveyed by the American Management Association, 81 percent offered free medical examinations to top management, while about 35 percent extended the offer to middle management.

Personal Time

In addition to physical well-being, your mental and emotional states are important elements in your overall health. A perk favored by many executives is one day a month of personal time. The day is spent away from the office in whatever activity or nonactivity the manager deems appropriate. The intent is to unwind from the stress and haste of business life and to recharge the psychic batteries. If the day is spent dashing about the city seeing your accountant about a tax problem, arguing with a department store manager about an overcharge, paying a parking fine at the Motor Vehicle Department, and arranging for a bank loan to pay a tuition bill, then little will have been done to ease the stress of everyday life. One favored activity is a drive to the beach or country where you can stroll slowly amid the quiet of forest or sand. A brief nap in the afternoon is usually a sign that the day is progressing nicely.

A day of reflection with sufficient time for careful sequential thought often produces a new approach to business problems or, at least, a less frenzied effort in solving them. Many executives find that it helps to get away for a day to examine their business life and its problems from a more contemplative perspective. Problems seem to assume more realistic proportions when viewed from a distance, and the annoyances and petty irritations of business life become more bearable.

Education

An extension of the perk of personal days is attendance at professional seminars. Getting away from the office for three or four days to attend the annual meeting of the Association of Corporate Finance Officers, or whatever your professional group is, can be beneficial. It provides an opportunity for travel and for experiencing new cities and different restaurants. If the meeting is well managed, it should add to one's professional growth by introducing new ideas or techniques. There is also the benefit of meeting with one's peers to exchange experiences or discuss mutual problems.

While professional conferences have their value, a manager should also seek out seminars or meetings that are not directly related to his work. There is a multitude of seminars going on at all times, sponsored by large organizations like the American Management Association; in addition, there are smaller meetings conducted by individual consultants. Many colleges and universities sponsor business seminars on their campuses, using faculty members and outside consultants. The University of Michigan, Stanford, Pace University in New York City, The University of Pittsburgh, and Washington University in the District of Columbia are especially active in this field. Seminar topics can range from managing stress to assertiveness training to memory skills to negotiation skills. There are, of course, many seminars that deal directly with specific business problems or situations that are of concern to managers. Some managers tend to avoid seminars, basing their reluctance on the belief that the time away from the office cannot be spared or that there is little to be learned away from the job. Both beliefs are erroneous. A seminar that is properly selected and competently conducted can be of great benefit both to the manager and his company. If it were not so, corporations would not continue to spend hundreds of millions of dollars each year on seminar expenses for their managers.

Legal Consultation

Here is a perk that everyone seems to find useful; many companies are beginning to offer it to managers other than corporate officers. Not to be outdone, unions are now starting to ask for the same privilege. General Motors recently signed a pact with the United Automobile Workers that included a new fund to provide legal assistance to the union members. The fund will be supported by a three-cents-an-hour contribution from the company. It is expected that the fund will be used by union members in their disputes over Social Security benefits, food stamps, traffic tickets, divorces, consumer complaints, property taxes, and IRS audits, to handle wills and home purchases, and to pay lawyers' fees in criminal actions. The fund cannot be used to sue General Motors, its dealers, or its unions, but it can be used to sue another automobile manufacturer—watch out, Toyota!

The knowledge and skills of the corporate legal department have always been available to the CEO and his closest aides. Now those same benefits are beginning to be distributed to those lower on the organization chart. The

AMA found that 18.6 percent of the companies surveyed provided some form of free legal counseling for their executives. Most of the legal services were in three areas: wills, estate planning, and real estate. Most of the companies that provide free legal advice allow their executives the option of using the company legal department, the law firm on retainer by the company, or an attorney of choice. None would bear the cost of court appearances by attorneys on behalf of a company employee. Only 2.6 percent of the surveyed companies extend the privilege below the vice presidential level, but there is no harm in asking. If you are rebuffed, you are no worse off than you were before.

Another course is to make a deliberate effort to get to know some of your company's legal staff. Find them at company meetings, social occasions, conventions, community service organizations, and elsewhere. You don't have to be on intimate terms to call a company lawyer and ask for a few minutes of his time; all you need are some previous encounters in which pleasantries were exchanged. State your problem as succinctly as possible and ask for advice. If your problem is outside his expertise, he will probably refer you to someone else in the department who has knowledge in that area. That is one of the advantages of a corporate legal staff; the range of knowledge is usually quite broad. It is an unusual problem that cannot be reviewed properly within a competent corporate legal group.

One note of caution. The company lawyer you consult is a company employee, so do not discuss anything you would not want known to your boss or the president. This is not to imply that company attorneys are eager to rush to the president with every hot little item they uncover, but their first loyalty is to the company, not to you. You are not the client of the company attorney; you are not paying him, and the privilege of attorney–client relationship does not exist. If, for example, you are under indictment for income tax evasion and somehow the story has not reached the newspapers, your best course of action is to seek legal counsel outside your company.

Personal Security

Not too many years ago, anyone so inclined could enter almost any office building in this nation and ask around until he located the personnel office or whatever person he might be looking for. Today, of course, things are much different. Corporate headquarters have become as difficult to enter as a Calvinist's heaven. The lobbies have uniformed guards barring access to the elevators and receptionists who require your signature before calling the person you have come to see. If approved, you are given a large visitor's pass to be visible at all times while you are in the building and returned to the receptionist when you depart. In some companies you are not allowed on the elevator alone, and the person you are calling on or his secretary must come and escort you to the proper office. The personnel offices that used to be on the third floor behind the cafeteria are now located just off the lobby so that job seekers need not wander about the premises.

The emphasis on increased corporate security began with the multinational corporations when their overseas employees and facilities came under attack. Factories and offices were bombed; executives were kidnapped or murdered. Bombings even began to occur within the continental United States, and stories circulated about terrorist plans to kidnap prominent American businessmen. The abduction of Patty Hearst was seen as an attack aimed at the Hearst Corporation, its nineteen-year-old heiress incidental to the main target. Shootings and kidnapping of European businessmen, especially in Germany and Italy, have become commonplace, and what was once seen only in other countries has become routine in America: corporate bodyguards.

Many U.S. companies now feel it necessary to provide

personal bodyguards for their top executives. Often the bodyguards serve a dual role as chauffeurs, but occasionally their only duty is to serve as a protective presence whenever the executive appears in public. The AMA study showed that 2.6 percent of the companies provided personal bodyguards for their executives; all the companies doing so were among the largest in America and presumably highly visible targets for terrorists or publicity seekers with a grievance. Most bodyguards are ex-policemen or soldier-of-fortune types who relish the risk involved. Most carry high-caliber handguns designed to create maximum noise and do maximum injury. Bodyguards who are assigned permanently to corporate executives are usually company employees with all the customary benefits. Often, however, a company will provide short-term protection for an executive making a public appearance before a congressional committee or a trade group or who, perhaps, has taken on an unusual assignment. The bodyguard is then hired from a security service such as Burns or Pinkerton. For many executives, personal security is a perk that has become a necessity.

An interesting addition has recently been seen in the bodyguard business: female bodyguards. They are employed by women executives who feel the need for someone at their side at all times. Female bodyguards undergo the standard training in martial arts, weapon use, and evasive driving and are considered to be as effective as men in any situation in which brute strength is not the primary need. Male executives are now beginning to ask for women bodyguards, preferring someone who is more unobtrusive than the highly visible bone-crusher type.

While a personal bodyguard may be a perk of little interest to you at this point, protecting your home against intruders is of concern to all of us. In the AMA study, 9.2 percent of the companies reported providing home security systems for selected executives. The reasoning is that a prominent executive of a major corporation, because of his position, becomes a more likely target of burglars, kidnappers, robbers, and mentally unstable individuals. Home security systems are usually selected by the company's director of security and installed under his supervision. They employ a variety of warning devices—taped windows and doors and/or ultrasound or microwave signals—to alert the homeowner. The systems are almost always tied in to the local police station or a private security service over a leased telephone line. When an intruder is detected, you have the option of a passive system that sends a signal over the phone line to summon help or an active system that also turns on lights and sets off a siren. The system will also be triggered if the phone line is cut.

7

Getting Financial Leverage

Passing a pet shop not long ago, I was captivated by the sight of a caged hamster busily galloping along on a circular treadmill. While I watched, the furry creature never deviated from his task, keeping the treadmill spinning at a splendid rate with no slackening of energy or interest. I admired the little fellow's persistence and thought of the life of a corporate manager. How many executives live in the same environment as the hamster? Our cages aren't as visible, but nevertheless they are there. Our tasks often seem as pointless and the rewards so meager as to cause outsiders to wonder what impels us to our incessant activity. When we have grown old and the energy to keep the wheel turning has lessened, we are allowed to rest—assuming we can find ease on the income provided by a pension that has been steadily eroded through inflation and by Social Security payments shakily based on ever higher taxes levied on fewer workers to provide for ever more recipients. At such a moment we look at the entrepreneurial spirits among us and wish we had taken our chances with a business of our own.

In a time when Elizabeth Taylor was only on her third marriage, I served a term as office boy to an insurance firm. I performed my duties so very well that soon I was allowed to sell. As an outside salesman I enjoyed a modicum of success that might have been greater had I not succumbed to a temptation unique to Chicago: daytime baseball. From my seat in the bleachers at Wrigley Field, the game was enlivened each day by a group of large, unshaven gentlemen in grimy undershirts who bet on the outcome of every pitch. Each bettor had a cigar in his mouth and in his hand a wad of bills as round as Liz's shapely calf. For some weeks I watched as vast sums of money changed hands at bewildering speed. In response to my query, the police officer assigned to the bleachers informed me that the bettors were all in the junk business and this was their way of spending an enjoyable afternoon. It was at that moment that I first became aware of the financial rewards of entrepreneurship. Unfortunately, my aversion to cigar smoke drove me back to the corporate world and I lost the opportunity to acquire significant monetary assets.

The typical corporate manager spends his career without ever managing to acquire much more cash than his furry compatriot on the treadmill. If he has accumulated a few shares of company stock and if it is worth more than he paid for it, he is both atypical and fortunate. His sole asset of any value is his home, and that will be of benefit only to his children when they sell it after his demise. Usually by then the mortgage has been paid off and the equity in the home represents a substantial sum, even when divided among the 2.4 children of the average family.

Lately, I have detected signs of rebellion against the unspoken assumption that it is the parents' duty to pass on the equity in their home to their children. Three friends of mine are taking a different approach. One plans to fully remortgage his house upon retirement and use the cash as a good-time fund. He and his wife have budgeted their expenditures for frivolity so that when they are seventy-five years old all the money will have been spent and they will have a fund of happy memories to reminisce over during the years left to them. If the house has appreciated further, they will sell it and move into an apartment with a second, smaller good-time fund to sustain them.

A second friend plans to sell his house and move to an apartment. All other assets will be converted to cash, added to the money from the sale of the house, and placed into a private foundation. While he and his wife are alive, the interest earned on their assets will be paid to them for their own use. Upon the death of both, the foundation will be converted to a trust fund for their descendants. The foundation will not pay benefits to the descendants but will serve as a source of funding for any family member who wishes to go into business for himself. The foundation will match dollar for dollar the capital provided by a descendant. The grant need not be repaid, but there will be a moral obligation to do so. The intent is to encourage the children and grandchildren to go into their own businesses, where the advantages of entrepreneurship can be enjoyed.

A third friend has a mortgage that is about halfway through its intended life. In return for a higher interest rate the bank has agreed that hereafter only interest payments need be made. My friend is now able to deduct 100 percent of his monthly payment on his income taxes and has added considerably to his cash flow through the deduction and the lower monthly payments. He, of course, is not building up any further equity in his home, but that will be a problem for his heirs, not him and his wife.

The reality for most executives is that upon retirement few will have liquid assets that will carry them more than a year or two. Their nightly prayers are for the solvency of Social Security and the control of inflation to maintain the buying power of their modest pension.

Nevertheless, it is possible for an executive to improve his financial position through other kinds of perks. You will never achieve the cash flow available to the owner of even a modest business, but the situation is not hopeless. Stock options, thrift plans, profit sharing, and low-interest loans offer avenues through which financial leverage can be secured and your cash position at retirement made significantly better. Astute financial counseling can enable you to use your assets wisely and allow you to emerge from your corporate career with more than a gold watch and a pat on the back.

Stock Options

Most publicly owned corporations set aside shares in the company for purchase by their executives. Typically, the options become available over a five-year period, with no more than twenty percent allowed to be converted in any one year. Usually, there are few restrictions on selling shares after they are acquired, but capital gains requirements often make it practical to hold stock for at least one year after its acquisition.

The purpose of stock options is twofold: first, to give an executive a vested interest in the success of his company and thereby motivate him to work more diligently; second, to allow him to reap some reward from the success of the company to which his work contributed.

Most companies make quite a to-do about the granting of options, and recipients are expected to be properly grateful. The gratitude is often quite genuine as managers soon have visions of country estates dancing in their heads when they calculate their expected capital gains. In 1967 I joined Xerox and was given an option to purchase two hundred shares of stock with additional shares to be available in future years. Xerox stock was then selling for $100 per share, which was my option price, and it had been doubling in value every two or three years for over a decade. My option shares were worth $20,000, and I skipped about my office in glee as I realized that if the value continued to increase as it had in the past, in another ten years they would be worth between $80,000 and $100,000. And that was only for the initial option shares; there would be more to follow! Leapin' lizards—I was going to be rich! (Followers of the stock market will not be surprised to learn I did not become rich: Xerox stock never again rose above $100 and my options never were exercised.)

From 1954 to 1969 the stock market went up and up and up and stock options were the hottest executive perk in town. Fortunes were made as executives exercised their options, cashed in their chips and, as a friend of mine did, bought a ranch at Big Sur on the Monterey Peninsula. The upsurge in stock prices leveled off in 1967 and then plunged downward in 1969. Many executives had to alter their plans for early retirement as LTV Corporation stock went from 170 to 15, Data Processing tumbled from 92 to 11, Parvin-Dohrmann sank from 142 to 19, Resorts International fell from 62 to 7, National Student Marketing dropped from 140 to 3, Transitron plunged from 60 to 10 and Four Seasons Nursing sold down from 91 to zero. Lest one think that precipitous declines affected only the cats and dogs, I offer the following from the stock tables of 1969–70:

Ten leading conglomerates down 86 percent (Litton, LTV, City Investing, Rapid-American, etc.)

Ten leading computer companies down 80 percent (IBM, Control Data, Sperry-Rand, Honeywell, etc.)

Ten leading technology companies down 77 percent (Polaroid, Xerox, Motorola, RCA, etc.)

It should come as no surprise that after the bottom fell out of the stock market in the late Sixties, stock options lost much of their appeal as a corporate perk. In terms of real, not inflated, dollars the market decline from 1969 to mid-1982 was as severe as the collapse from 1929 to 1932. After adjusting for inflation, the Dow-Jones Industrial Average in mid-1982 was 68-percent below where it stood in the late 1960s. Many solid companies had shares selling at the lowest price/earnings ratio in their history. During the 1950s and 1960s the average P/E ratio of the Dow-Jones Industrials was consistently above 15. Growth stocks such as IBM, Litton, Fairchild, Xerox, ITT, RCA, Polaroid, and Raytheon sold anywhere from fifty to one hundred times earnings. As of mid-1982 those same stocks had the following price/earnings ratios:

IBM	5.6
Litton	4.2
Fairchild	5.9

Xerox	9.6
ITT	11.1
RCA	4.6
Polaroid	5.3
Raytheon	4.3

Although the Dow-Jones Industrial Average has risen to over 1,000, the stock of the average company today represents a bargain that will not be seen again until the next stock-market bust. A well-managed, well-financed company today offers little or no risk of substantial decline in the price of the stock.

What does this all mean for a program to gain financial leverage? First, you should not ignore stock options or accord them little value. Second, you do not want to be in a position where you are forced to exercise your options before it is advantageous. There is no sense in paying for company stock that may not appreciate in value for some years. The time to exercise an option is after the price of the stock has risen substantially above your option price. Remember, your stock price is locked in; you don't have to worry about buying before the crowd drives the price up. You can afford to keep your cash in a money market fund or similar income-producing account until the last minute.

When you do exercise your option, mark off the capital gains date on your calendar. Each day after the capital gains date you should consider selling your stock. As long as the market and your stock is continuing to rise, there is, of course, no reason to sell. But someday your stock will start to fall and it will be time to sell. If the market recovers, you can buy back in. If the market continues to fall, you will have locked in your profit and can put the money into Treasury certificates. Others, holding onto their stock and looking for the big killing, will watch as their assets disappear.

The Tax Reform Act of 1981 both simplified and complicated the handling of stock options. Options acquired prior to May 1981 but exercised after that date will have to be handled carefully. These are governed by the tax acts of 1964 and 1976, under which companies could grant their employees "qualified stock options." These, if certain criteria were met, allowed an employee to treat the profit from his options as a capital gain. In order to qualify, the options had to be granted at the closing price of the stock as of the day of grant; the employee had a maximum of five years in which to exercise his options and then had to hold them for three years before selling.

Many companies thought these restrictions too confining and simply granted options under terms they thought best, forcing the employees to treat their profits as ordinary income on their tax returns. In many cases the employees came out better than if they had had to conform to all the restrictions of "qualified" options. The principal problem was that an employee had to pay taxes on whatever profit existed at the time the options were exercised, even though the shares had not been sold and an actual profit created.

An employee whose stock was still appreciating in value faced a dilemma. If he sold some of the stock to pay the additional taxes, he would lose the benefit of a rising market in his company's stock. The solution for many was to take out a loan using the stock as collateral. Profits were preserved, but monthly expenses were increased—not an ideal situation. A worse situation arose for an employee who exercised his options, paid the taxes on his paper profit, and then watched as the stock price declined before he sold. In effect, he had paid taxes on profits that never existed; he would, of course, have a deduction when he eventually sold the stock, but that was small comfort.

Under the Tax Reform Act of 1981, you do not have to pay taxes on any profits until the shares of stock have actually been sold. In addition, if the shares are held for one year after purchase, the profit will be taxed at the capital gains rate. These two changes, combined with a reduction in the tax rate on capital gains, makes stock options much more attractive than they had been.

Two additional requirements must be met to qualify for

capital gains treatment on your profit. You must wait two years after the option is granted before exercising it, and you must still be working for the company at least three months before the option is exercised. This last proviso means that if you are nearing retirement, you should exercise all your options before going off the company payroll. Unless all these provisions are met, profits will be taxed as ordinary income.

The Tax Act of 1982 created a new alternative minimum tax that principally affects taxpayers with large capital gains or unusually high itemized deductions. The first $30,000 of alternative-minimum-taxable income is exempt from the tax ($40,000 for joint returns). Income subject to the tax above those amounts is taxed at a flat rate of 20 percent.

The problem you may face if you exercise a stock option is that your paper profit must be added to other capital gains to determine if you will come under the new alternative minimum tax. To illustrate: let's suppose you own options on 1,000 shares of company stock at $10.00 per share. You exercise the options on a day that the stock trades for $20.00 per share. You now have a paper profit of $10,000. That amount must be added to other capital gains to determine if you are subject to the new alternative minimum tax.

In structuring an option plan the company must meet certain requirements to ensure that profits will be treated as capital gains. Check these out with a prospective employer:

1. Shareholders must approve the plan within twelve months and options must be granted within ten years.
2. The total number of shares available must be specified.
3. All eligible employees must be specified. This need not be by name but can be by title or job level.
4. Options may not be transferred except to a beneficiary upon the death of the holder.
5. Options must be exercised within ten years of their

being granted or five years if the grantee owns more than 10 percent of the company stock.

6. The price of the option should be the closing price as of the date of issuance. The price must be 10-percent higher than the closing price for grantees who own more than 10 percent of the company stock.

7. If there is more than one option, they must be exercised in the order granted.

8. Only $100,000 of options in any one year per employee is eligible for favored tax treatment but half of any unused grant in a year may be carried forward for up to three years.

A company has complete freedom in creating option plans, but unless it meets the qualifications listed above, all profits will be treated as ordinary income. If you have options granted after January 1, 1976, you may still qualify for the new tax treatment of your profits so long as you meet all the requirements of the new act.

This section, and others dealing with tax matters are not intended as definitive treatments of present tax laws. The complexity of our tax system makes that impossible. In addition, tax laws and decisions by tax courts are constantly changing. Before making any decisions involving tax matters, you should consult with a capable tax specialist.

The American Management Associations surveyed 400 companies, mostly medium-sized, about their stock-option plans and found that among those companies options had been granted to 1,909 executives, an average of fewer than five executives per company. However, the options reached surprisingly far down into management ranks, with 189 managers in the $10,000 to $20,000 salary group receiving options. The following table summarizes the AMA study, published in 1982, and offers an opportunity to see how your company's option plan stacks up against the average of the companies surveyed.

VALUE OF STOCK OPTIONS GRANTED

Salary Group	Number of Executives in Group	Average Value of Options
More than $200,000	26	$371,615
100,000– 200,000	190	177,768
90,000– 100,000	46	172,695
80,000– 90,000	80	119,800
70,000– 80,000	98	101,765
60,000– 70,000	132	83,773
50,000– 60,000	193	73,813
40,000– 50,000	253	55,992
30,000– 40,000	343	40,412
20,000– 30,000	359	20,863
10,000– 20,000	189	11,232

If your company does not have an incentive stock option plan, it is in the minority of American businesses, at least among the larger companies. The Tax Reform Act of 1981 has encouraged many companies that had not previously done so to provide stock options. A survey of 200 prominent corporations by Towers, Perrin, Forster & Crosby showed that 85 percent plan to offer stock options in the near future. The company also studied the 1981 proxy statements of two-thirds of the hundred largest companies and found that 52 percent had already adopted a stock-option plan. In addition, more than 60 percent of the companies surveyed said they were planning to convert their nonqualified option plans into new incentive stock-option plans. However, 13 percent of the companies said they did not plan to convert their stock-option plans because under the new plans a company loses a valuable tax deduction.

Congress wrote incentive stock options into the Tax Reform Act of 1981 in order to encourage companies to provide the benefit to key employees. This was done to afford corporate managers an opportunity to acquire assets almost impossible to obtain on their salaries alone. If the response of the companies surveyed is indicative of most American corporations, Congress's intent is being fulfilled.

In addition to ordinary stock-option plans there are a number of variations that companies have devised.

APPRECIATION GRANTS

An employee is listed as owning a certain number of shares as of a specific date, with a termination date for the ownership. If the stock has risen in value on the termination date, the employee is given the amount of the appreciation in either cash or company stock. The termination date can be set anywhere from six months to ten years or more into the future. This is another form of "golden handcuffs" and serves to keep an employee on the payroll until the termination date, assuming there has been an increase of significance in the value of the stock.

PHANTOM STOCK OPTIONS

These are similar to appreciation grants except there is no specific termination date. The grants can run anywhere from one year to ten years or more. The usual period is three to five years. An employee decides when to exercise his options and is paid in either cash or company stock for whatever appreciation in value has occurred. This option can be just as "golden" as the one above, but there is less of a "handcuff" effect.

FORMULA VALUE GRANTS

These are similar to phantom grants except that a formula is used to determine the value of the cash or stock paid out. The formula can either increase or decrease the actual appreciation of the stock. The factors that make up the formula can be based on company rank, performance criteria, time with the company, or any of a multitude of other factors considered significant. Working for a company under this option requires not only a calculation of how much the stock is worth but how the formula will affect the payoff. If the factors making up the formula are beyond your control, such as company profits or return on investment or increase in shareholders' equity, all you can do is hang in there and hope things work out. If the factors involve your performance, for example, operating costs for your department or productivity increasing, then you should focus on those aspects of your job in order to weight the formula in your favor.

FULL-VALUE GRANTS

These are simple gifts of shares of company stock. It is the same as a bonus except that it comes in the form of stock. The criteria for determining performance bonuses are usually applied in the same way for full-value grants.

The obvious purpose of all the variations on basic stock options is to provide the advantages of options without requiring employees to pay out the cash necessary to exercise a stock option. As such, the variations meet with considerable approval from managers on a first-name basis with the local orthodontist or with an offspring about to enter college.

Some guidelines to remember after acquiring your stock:

Falling in love with a stock is fatal.
A stock that goes up will come down.
There is no such thing as a paper profit; you haven't won until you cash in your chips.

There is a saying on Wall Street that is instructive: "A bear can make money and a bull can make money, but a pig, never!"

Low-Interest Loans

Now that you have your options and the stock price has risen handsomely, where do you get the money to exercise your options? The stock may now be worth $100,000 and you can buy it for $50,000, but how do you come up with the 50K? If you want to put up the stock as collateral, a bank will be happy to lend you the $50,000 at 15-percent interest. Just paying back the interest will cost you upwards of $600 a month. You could refinance the mortgage on your house; that will lower your interest payments a bit but leave you saddled with a higher mortgage rate. It's time to do what many managers are doing: get a low-interest loan from your company.

This is a perk of fairly recent popularity brought about by inflation and interest rates at historic highs. Not too many years ago, home mortgages were available at less than 7 percent and personal loans were made at less than 10 percent. In those days, a company might occasionally guarantee a loan for an employee, but interest rates were so low that it was not thought necessary for a company to make the actual loan. *Forbes* magazine recently pointed out that interest rates in recent times were higher than at any time since Christ walked the earth. Under such circumstances many companies find it necessary to make loans to their executives at interest rates of 4 or 5 percent, which are closer to historic rates than the current inflated rates. Some even charge no interest if the loan is to a CEO or his one or two top executives. Below that level, interest is almost always charged.

The AMA study showed that 6.2 percent of the companies made loans to their executives at less than the market rate and another 5.2 percent arranged to have the firm's bank make loans at favorable terms. There were also 6.2 percent of the companies who made loans at no interest rate at all; again, unfortunately, the names are not revealed. The duration of the loans ranged from less than one year up to ten years. In about half the companies, the loan becomes due upon termination; the others either continue the terms or schedule a shorter payback period.

This is one perk in which banks and other financial institutions surpass their counterparts in industry. More than

10 percent of the banks responding to the survey reported making loans at less than the going rate for certain executives. Personal experience leads me to believe that that percentage is substantially short of the actual number of banks that provide this service to their top people. In addition, a careful reading of financial statements supplied by bankers appointed to high-level government positions almost always reveals personal loans from their banks at favorable rates. In banking, low-cost loans are considered the same type of professional perk as allowing managers of consumer products companies to purchase the company's products at a discount.

In West Germany, company loans are a firmly established perk offered by almost every company of any size, and, in fact, the tax laws encourage such loans. If the interest rate on the loan is 4 percent or higher, or if the loan is for DM 5,000 or less, there is no tax liability to the employee. Also, if the loan is for the purchase of a home, it is tax-free regardless of the interest rate or the amount.

Company loans are made to enable an executive to exercise stock options, to purchase a home, to deal with an emergency, to buy an automobile, or simply to take advantage of an investment opportunity. The advantage to the company is that the loan becomes another form of "golden handcuffs" that further ties the employee to the company. The advantage to the employee is that he now has money borrowed at an interest rate that is financially advantageous. The terms of the loan are a matter of negotiation between the company and the employee. The interest rate can range from none to a point or two below the market rate. Some loans have a regular payback schedule, as with a mortgage. Others require that only the interest be paid until the end of the time period when the balance is due. Still others do not require any payment until the end, when the entire balance and interest is due. Some compound the interest; others do not. Obviously, you should try to structure the loan to your best advantage.

Sit down with your accountant ahead of time and determine what type of loan would be most helpful to you and what terms would be least punishing. Then, when you enter the negotiations, you will have a clear picture of your needs and be in a much better position to realize them.

Even if you are not buying a home or exercising stock options, you should give serious consideration to arranging a low-interest loan with your company. Let's suppose you borrow $50,000 from your company at 5-percent interest, compounded annually and the full amount of principal and interest payable at the end of five years. At that time you will have to come up with $63,814 ($50,000 loan plus accrued interest of $13,814.). If you take the $50,000 and put it into a bank certificate of deposit paying 9 percent, compounded monthly, at the end of five years you will have earned $30,626 in interest. After paying off the loan and the accrued interest, your profit would be $16,812, less the additional income tax you would have paid over the five years on the interest earned each year. However, your interest payment of $13,814 is made in one year and is deducted from only one year's income, providing considerable leverage over the interest income that you spread over five years. After credits and debits you would have added approximately $20,000, or $5,000 per year, to your income and, best of all, it would be available at the end of five years in a lump sum rather than having been spent.

You could have achieved the same result by rolling over 30-day Treasury certificates. In either case, the investment would have been at no risk. If you are willing to take a modest risk, the returns can be greater. Let's assume you believe that before the five years have passed interest rates will come down. If the rates do come down, bond prices will go up. Therefore, you decide to buy Treasury bonds with your $50,000. Many are now available paying 10-percent interest. Without any compounding, at the end of five years you will have earned $25,000 in interest. If you take the semiannual interest payments of $2,500 and invest them in 8-percent 30-day Treasury certificates, you'd earn an additional $2,515 during the five years. Without any increase in the value of the bond, you'll have earned $27,515 in interest. Subtracting the interest of $13,814 that you owe leaves a profit of $13,701—again, less the additional income taxes you paid as you received your interest on the bonds and Treasury bills.

If your assumption about a decline in interest rates was correct, a capital gain on the value of your bonds will be available to you. Let's assume that the interest rates decline from 10 to 8 percent over the five years. Your bonds would have increased in value by about 30 percent (the gain is greater than the actual percentage decline in interest rates). This provides a capital gain on the value of the bonds of approximately $15,000. Of that profit, $9,200 (60 percent) is excluded from your taxable income. The remaining $6,000 (40 percent) is added to your taxable income for that year and taxed at your normal rate. Even if you are in the highest tax bracket of 50 percent, you end up paying a tax of only $3,000 on a profit of $15,000. In addition, you have a tax writeoff of $13,814, which will save almost $7,000 on your total tax obligation for the year.

On that basis, your total return on the borrowed $50,000 would be as follows:

Bond interest earned over five years	$25,000
Interest earned on bond interest	2,515
Net capital gain	15,000
50 percent tax saving on $13,814 of interest paid	6,907
Total investment return	$49,422

Of course, over the five years you would have had to pay taxes on the interest you earned each year. However, those interest earnings would have been spread over five years, so the cumulative effect on your tax liabilities would not have been too great.

You must remember that the second investment strategy involves some risk. Interest rates may not come down over the next five years. Or they may come down and then go up again just before the five years are up and the loan has to be repaid. Persons who bought Treasury notes paying 8¾-percent interest and due in November 1988 will lose almost 20 percent of their investment if they have to sell as of this writing (mid-1982). Interest rates have gone up since those notes were issued, depressing the value of the notes. You have to balance the risk against the probable return.

The operative word in the last sentence above is "risk." Even Treasury securities involve the risk of devaluation through inflation. Here are two stories from the business pages to illustrate the risks involved in loans and their use.

When Archie McCardell left Xerox in 1977 to join International Harvester as CEO, he was given a loan of $1.5 million at 6-percent interest with which to buy IH stock. At that time IH stock was being traded at $30, which was near the bottom of its trading range in the near past. In addition to the loan, a formula was devised to measure the company's performance against six leading competitors. If IH did better than average, the board had the option of forgiving up to 25 percent of the loan in any one year. McCardell's first full year, 1978, left the board underwhelmed, and nothing was done about the loan. However, 1979 was a different story; the board was so pleased with the company's results, still mediocre by John Deere standards, that it forgave the entire loan. In order to comply with the terms of the agreement, the forgiving was to take place in five equal installments over the next five years. At that point the stock had risen just above $40 a share and McCardell had himself a paper profit of a half million or so, which, added to the written-off loan, put him $2 million ahead of the game. Alas, the game turned sour, and by the end of 1981, IH stock had fallen below $5 a share. The company was facing bankruptcy, the unions were being asked to make wage concessions, and McCardell had a paper loss of approximately $1.3 million. The board called off the whole deal, and Archie resigned.

Richard Black had carved out an enviable career at Maremont and in February 1981 moved on to bigger and better things as CEO of AM International. As part of his compensation package AM loaned him $1.6 million at 6-percent interest to buy company stock, and Black added $1.6 million of his own money to the stock purchase. The stock was bought at $$11.12 a share, and the loan was to be repaid in two equal installments of $834,375 on March 17, 1985, and March 17, 1986. Black resigned after one year with AM and filed suit against the company for more than $3 million, claiming the company gave him misleading financial information prior to his employment. The company has since placed itself under the protection of a Chapter 11 bankruptcy. Black's case has been lumped with a dozen others in a class action, the end of which is not to be known for some time.

The moral of these two tales is that borrowed money is a wonderful invention, but only when it is used wisely. McCardell and Black would probably testify that there are safer investments than purchasing company stock with borrowed money.

Thrift Plans

In November of 1981 the Internal Revenue Service issued proposed regulations that clarified the establishment of thrift plans and their tax consequences. The regulations are not final, but many companies have decided to offer the plans to their employees immediately; others, however, are waiting for final regulations.

Thrift plans are designed for the same purpose as Individual Retirement Accounts (IRAs): offering people an opportunity to provide for their own financial security during retirement. There are at least four significant advantages to thrift plans over IRAs:

1. Contributions made by an employee are usually matched, all or in part, by the employer.
2. There is no limit to the amount an employee can put into a thrift plan.

3. There is no penalty for withdrawing money before age 59½, providing it is done for "hardship" reasons.
4. Money paid out of a thrift plan is eligible for ten-year averaging rather than being taxed at regular rates.

None of this is to imply that if you have a thrift plan you needn't bother with an IRA. Both plans provide valuable leverage in your struggle for financial independence, and both should be used to the fullest.

Most companies that have thrift plans allow their employees to set aside a specific percentage of each paycheck into the plan. Taxes are paid on the money that is set aside, but once the money is invested, no taxes are paid on the appreciation until monies are paid out. Most companies allow between 5 and 10 percent of an employee's income to be automatically paid into a thrift plan. The company then matches all or part of the employees' contribution, usually half of the first 5 percent. Phillips Petroleum stockholders recently approved a proposal to have the company match employees' contributions dollar for dollar. Sherwin-Williams employees can have up to 20 percent of their pay used to buy company stock, and S-W matches dollar for dollar.

Usually, an employee had at least two choices, and often three, as to how his money will be invested. The choices are a fixed income account, a mutual stock fund, or purchase of company stock. The money can also be spread among the choices to provide diversification. The money can be moved from one account to another, but usually no more than once a year.

If you leave before retirement, you receive back all you paid into the account. In order to be fully vested in the company's contribution, you usually must stay five years, with 20-percent vesting occurring each year. If you leave a company and receive a lump-sum payment from your thrift account, your contributions have already been taxed; the company's contributions, plus appreciation, are eligible for ten-year averaging.

Some quick calculations can show the value of a thrift plan. Let's assume you are earning $30,000 a year and put 10 percent into a thrift plan with the company matching half your contribution. Assuming no increases in pay, each year $4,500 is going into your account. If the funds earn a modest 10 percent, your account will grow as follows:

End of Year	Account Value
1	$ 4,500
2	9,450
3	14,895
4	20,885
5	27,473
10	71,718
15	142,976
20	257,738

Actually, the value at the end of each year would be somewhat higher than is shown, because the money would have been invested over the course of each year rather than in one lump sum at the end of each year. Interest calculated monthly would also have been earned during each year and would have increased the totals shown.

The table above is another testament to the power of compound interest and the effects of a regular, sustained savings program. The Reagan administration has committed itself to raising the savings rate of American families in an effort to provide more funds for industrial expansion. IRAs, Keoghs, thrift plans, and incentive stock options are all part of that strategy. If your company is not participating in the latter two, perhaps you should prod them a little to get into line with current economic thinking.

Deferred Compensation

There are no recent studies of the frequency with which companies allow their executives to defer part of their salaries, but it is fairly common at the upper levels of major corporations. Not too many companies extend the privilege below the level of senior vice president, but Honeywell has what it calls a "pay-conversion plan," in which more than half their employees participate. In other companies, it is known as a "salary-reduction plan" or a "deferred compensation plan." By any name, the purpose of such plans is to reduce an employee's taxable income and add to the employee's retirement assets.

The pay-conversion plan at Honeywell is a relatively new venture approved by the IRS, and a number of other companies are studying it. At Honeywell, employees can participate in one or both of two deferred compensation plans. The first is called "Pay-Conversion Contributions" and allows an employee to have 4 percent of his income put into a retirement account. The second is called "Tax-Deductible Contributions" and allows up to $2,000 annually to be set aside. The Honeywell plans are similar to thrift plans in that the money is invested in either a fixed-income fund, a stock and bond fund, or an equity fund indexed to the Standard and Poor's 500. The money cannot be withdrawn until age 59½.

The Honeywell program differs from a thrift plan in two ways:

1. The company does not contribute to the plan.
2. Monies paid into the plan are not taxed until withdrawn.

The great advantage of course is that funds are being deposited, as in an IRA or Keogh, which are not subject to current taxes. Honeywell has computed the growth in the value of the plans over a period of time. Assume that you are earning $20,000 per year, receive pay increases of 8 percent annually, and contribute 4 percent plus $2,000 each year. With no withdrawals and an investment return of 10 percent a year, the growth would be as follows:

Years of Participation	Total Contributions	Total Investment Earnings	Total Before-tax Account Growth
10	$ 31,589	$ 22,605	$ 54,194
20	76,610	140,323	216,933
30	150,627	536,277	686,904

The Honeywell plan and others similar to it stem from one of the provisions of the Tax Reform Act of 1978. As a result of the act it became possible for the first time for a company to structure a savings plan in which the money set aside would not be part of an employee's taxable income. Nothing was done to take advantage of this provision until late 1981 when the IRS finally issued its proposed regulations. Most companies are still waiting to act, but Honeywell and a few other hardy souls have plunged in.

If your company does not now have a deferred compensation plan, it may soon create one. There are significant advantages to deferred compensation over thrift plans or IRAs. *Business Week* says that deferred compensation is about to become the hottest thing in benefits administration. Under IRS regulations employees can have up to 6 percent of their gross income taken off the top and placed in a deferred compensation plan. Since all the money in the plan is yours, you are fully vested at all times. The money must remain in the plan until one of three things occur:

1. You reach age 59½ or later and withdraw the money, all or in part. Payments are then subject to normal income tax at your regular rate. However, the payments are eligible for ten-year averaging, which should reduce the tax bite considerably.
2. You leave the company and the money is paid to you in a lump sum. At that time you can retain the money and pay taxes on it, again using the ten-year averaging. You also have the option to avoid imme-

113

diate taxes on the money by rolling it over into a similar plan at your new employer or placing it in your IRA. If it is placed in your IRA, it is commingled with those funds, which are then eligible for only five-year averaging upon withdrawal.
3. You die and the money becomes part of your estate, subject to whatever taxes might be levied upon the estate.

A nice feature of deferred-compensation plans is that your employer must continue to calculate your pension, insurance, and health benefits on the basis of your full salary.

There are two other ways of getting money out of a deferred-compensation plan:

1. You can request a withdrawal on the basis of "hardship." In the past the IRS usually has interpreted this to mean that the money is needed to purchase a house, pay tuition expenses, or meet medical costs not covered by your company's health plan.
2. You can borrow money from your deferred-compensation plan so long as you pay it back on a regular schedule and at a reasonable rate of interest.

At a different level, it has been common for many years for top managers to defer part of their income until retirement, when the tax bite is less severe. The deferred salary can be handled in a number of ways. The simplest is when the company agrees to start paying a certain sum each year after a specific date for a stated number of years. In effect, the manager has deferred part of his current income to maintain part of his salary beyond retirement. A company likes such a plan because it can either place the deferred amounts in interest-bearing accounts that earn additional income for the company or set up a reserve, which is really a paper transaction allowing use of the money.

If you are not certain of your company's ability to pay your deferred compensation far into the future, you can ask that an annuity be purchased to guarantee such payments—a wise move for managers at International Harvester or AM International.

Financial Counseling

Personnel Journal says this is the hottest perk in town: not that so many companies are offering it but that so many managers are asking for it. Anyone with even a few thousand dollars of savings has to be bewildered by the opportunities available for the investment of his money. Where do we put our money? In an IRA, a company thrift plan, deferred compensation, a money market account, an all-saver's certificate, the exercise of stock options, or parts of some or all of the above? One thing we all know is that funds should not be left in a bank earning 5¼-percent interest when a simple money market fund with easy access to our money will pay more than 8 percent.

For those at or near the 50-percent tax bracket, the choices become even greater. Is it time to start thinking about tax shelters? If so, which ones—oil and gas drilling programs, real estate investment trusts, herds of cattle, or, as a friend of mine does, porno movies? My friend is in the 50-percent tax bracket and twice a year provides $10,000 to finance "quality" (sic) porno flicks. Each $10,000 is written off his taxes and fifteen months later is returned to him by the film's producer. The tax writeoff takes advantage of provisions in the tax laws for rapid depreciation of master copies of films, and the $10,000 returned to him is considered a return of original investment, which in a partnership is nontaxable. The net is that over a fifteen-month period he realizes a 50-percent return on each investment. It's not as respectable as a Christmas Club account at Chase Manhattan, but the results are eminently satisfying.

So, here you are, a successful corporate manager earning a decent living. Perhaps your spouse is also working and for the first time you have more than a few bucks between you and the relief rolls. You got burned in the stock market in the late Sixties and you don't want to try that again. Mutual funds haven't been going anywhere for the past four years so that investment route doesn't appeal to you. You've heard all about new investment opportunities but you don't have the time or the financial acumen to be able to sort them out. You decide to consult a financial planner and discover that his advice is so expensive that even at a 20-percent annual return it will be a few years before you earn back the fee you paid to the expert. You turn to the guy who does your taxes and if you're lucky he tells you to put your money into an IRA and everything left over into a money market fund.

If you're not lucky he tells you about a hot new venture to open a chain of acne clinics all across the country. It's going to be the biggest thing since McDonald's! "Every teenager in the country's got zits, right! We got a guaranteed treatment that'll clear up that pizza look. We charge 'em forty bucks a visit and they get a treatment every week for six weeks, now we're talkin' about big bucks, baby, big bucks! The best part is every year we got a new crop of zit-faced fourteen-year-olds who want to score with the chick in biology class! Baby, I'm tellin' you in three years the $25,000 you're puttin' into this is gonna be a million. Whatta you say?"

If you're smart you say, "Uh, excuse me, but I'm double-parked. Gotta run."

Now it's time to turn to the storehouse of financial wisdom abiding within the bosom of your company. If you're the CEO you've been doing it for years. You don't have time to look after your finances; other people do that for you. The other people may be inside or outside the company but wherever they are, you aren't paying for it. The American Management Association survey shows that 36 percent of the companies responding provided free financial services to their executives. Sixteen percent of the companies providing the perk did so with company staff members, 17 percent with outside firms on retainer to the company, 9 percent with consultants of the executive's choice, and 7 percent other.

While 36 percent of the companies provided free financial services to their CEOs, only 4.8 percent provided similar services to their middle management. American Can is an exception, paying half the cost of a financial planning service for all their employees. The company and the employee split the $96 cost and the employee, after providing confidential information, receives a 28-page printout analyzing his personal finances, prepared by the Consumer Financial Institute of Newton, Massachusetts, and designed to show the realities of a family's financial situation and suggest alternatives and strategies. CFI makes a point of being independent in their recommendations since they do not sell insurance, tax shelters, or other products.

This last issue may be important in evaluating the advice you receive from a financial advisor. There are many financial consultants who insist that their recommendations are totally objective even though they may be acting as a broker in recommending the purchase of insurance or tax shelters or the like. They claim, with some vehemence, that they could not long remain in the business if their recommendations were not only objective but beneficial. In many cases this is undoubtedly so, but the opportunity for abuse exists and, given the weaknesses of human nature, if an opportunity exists, it will be taken by some.

While a step in the right direction, American Can's program hardly compares with the free services provided by many companies to their CEOs and top managers. Among those companies the cost of outside financial counseling averaged $1,552 per executive. In the insurance industry, where financial planning is apparently well-regarded, the average cost per executive was $2,413.

Most companies prefer that the executive go elsewhere for his financial advice; if his investments turn sour, no one wants a company executive weeping on the desk of the company financial officer who got him into that sure thing in pork-belly futures.

Companies that specialize in financial planning for executives begin with a meeting with the executive and spouse. At that meeting a complete picture is obtained of the couple's financial situation including assets, liabilities, cash flow, credit potential, insurance coverage, company benefits, and present investments. A second meeting is usually held at which the executive and spouse receive a complete report on their financial situation. The couple is then queried as to its known financial obligations in the future, such as college expenses or caring for a parent. A discussion is held as to the financial objectives of the couple and the reasons for those objectives. A third meeting is then held to present recommendations as to how the objectives can be met or scaled down to realistic limits. After that, there is often a yearly conference to update the data and track progress in achieving the couple's financial objectives.

8

Finessing the Tax Man

The preceding chapter was devoted to ways in which you can use the tax laws to provide a better financial future for yourself. In business parlance this is known as *long-range planning,* a term honored more in the breach than in the observance. Aside from a few exemplars such as IBM or General Electric, five-year plans at most companies are done with the same expectations as wishes made before candles are blown out on a birthday cake. But, as General Eisenhower once remarked, it's not the plan that matters; it's the planning.

Which calls to mind a friend who was having lunch with one of the venture capitalists on Wall Street. My friend had a small struggling business in a high-tech area that seemed to have some potential. If the business was to grow, it would need an infusion of investment capital; that was the purpose of the lunch. After a discussion of the company's history and prospects, the venture capitalist asked, "I'd like to take a look at your five-year plan, if I might."

My friend replied, "I'd be happy to provide it, but we don't have one."

The venture capitalist asked, "Well, could you describe your long-range plan?"

"My long-range plan is to meet the payroll this Friday."

"Good grief, what's your short-range plan?"

"Figuring out who's going to pay for this lunch."

Most of us are like my friend, but things need not be so.

As a corporate manager there are ways in which you can significantly improve your short-term financial situation. You do not have the advantage of owning a small business and thereby writing off ordinary living expenses, but as a corporate employee there are many everyday costs that can be shifted to your company. The goal is to not change your lifestyle but to transfer some of your living expenses. In that way, you are not spending after-tax dollars for some of your living costs and the company gets a tax deduction for its expenses on your behalf. Everybody benefits but the tax man, which is how the game is played under the world's most complicated tax system. Let's look at some of the relevant perks.

Company Car

As has often been said, Americans have a love affair with the automobile. And, as any lover can attest, in a love affair costs are not a consideration. Few Americans know the real costs of owning an automobile. We love our cars and we don't compute the costs any more than we do for our children. The truth is that owning a car has become a luxury and the financial straits that many families find themselves in is due to their habit of buying a new car every three or four years. Anyone who does not have to drive to work does not need a car; it's as simple as that. Which means that anywhere from one-third to one-half the families in America could sell their cars tomorrow and be better off never buying another. The major sufferers would be the auto makers, but think what it would do for our balance of payments with Japan.

The Hertz Corporation publishes an annual report on the cost of owning an automobile in various cities around the nation. The study published in February 1982 and covering the calendar year of 1981 showed that the cost per mile of owning a car had risen by 50 percent in the preceding two years. While not unbiased, Hertz's annual figures have never been seriously challenged. Hertz bases its figures on cars that are owned for four years and driven an average of 10,000 miles per year. Average purchase prices are obtained for each category of cars in each city, and city variations are also used in calculating the costs of depreciation, insurance, licenses, fees, maintenance, repairs, gasoline, oil, and other service station charges.

HERTZ ESTIMATE OF THE ANNUAL COST OF OWNING AN AUTOMOBILE

City	Compact	Intermediate	Full-Size
Los Angeles	$5,850	$6,364	$6,636
New York City	5,662	6,229	6,495
San Francisco	5,629	6,192	6,457
Miami	4,968	5,465	5,699
Chicago	4,854	5,340	5,568
Seattle	4,760	5,236	5,461
Houston	4,653	5,119	5,338
St. Louis	4,649	5,114	5,333
Denver	4,646	5,111	5,330
San Diego	4,637	5,101	5,319
Boston	4,634	5,098	5,316
Minneapolis	4,591	5,050	5,267
Milwaukee	4,585	5,044	5,260
Pittsburgh	4,571	5,028	5,244
Cleveland	4,497	4,947	5,159
District of Columbia	4,463	4,910	5,120
Dallas	4,358	4,794	4,999
Atlanta	4,358	4,684	4,885
Cincinnati	4,286	4,715	4,917
Detroit	4,195	4,615	4,812

The costs above do not include parking or tolls. For city dwellers in Manhattan, San Francisco, and Boston, parking costs can add anywhere from $50 to $150 per month. If you drive to work in any of the major cities of the Northeast, tolls can add another $500 or so each year to your automobile expenses.

How much do you have to earn to pay for your beloved automobile? That depends on your tax bracket. Here is a chart to help you determine how much of your income goes to your car, when the average annual cost of an intermediate car is $5,208:

Taxable Income	Marginal Tax Rate	Gross Income Needed
11,800–15,000	22%	$6,677
15,001–18,200	23%	6,764
18,201–23,500	28%	7,233
23,501–28,800	32%	7,659
28,801–34,100	38%	8,400
34,101–44,700	41%	8,828
44,701–60,600	49%	10,212
60,601 and up	50%	10,416

The chart above shows the true value to you of a company car. If the company does not now provide you with a car, at your next salary review you could ask for a car instead of the first $5,000 of your increase; you'll still come out ahead. Even if you had to pay for the gas and oil, it would be to your advantage to drive a company-owned car.

The AMA survey showed that 83 percent of the companies responding provided company cars for their executives and only 10 percent insisted that the car be primarily for business use. Company cars are most common for CEOs and top managers, but approximately 10 percent of the companies also provide cars for selected middle managers. CEOs usually get Lincolns or Cadillacs, while top managers get Buicks or Chryslers, and middle managers get Fords or Chevrolets. A compact car is considered more an insult than a perk. Assuming your company provides you with a car, there is a financial advantage only if it replaces a present car. If you previously had one car and now keep two, you are no better off. Aside from the annual cost of owning an automobile, there is the cost of being unable to invest the money you have tied up in your car. That cost can be considerable, as the following table shows.

The table is based on the assumption that you own an intermediate car and its annual after-tax cost to you is $5,000. You are provided with a company car and sell your old car, which frees up $5,000 annually for investment. You put the money into tax-free municipal bonds paying a modest 10 percent and reinvest the annual dividends of $500. Here is how a $5,000 annual investment will grow over a period of years:

End of Year	Total Investment	Accumulated Interest	Value of Investment
1	$ 5,000	500	$ 5,500
2	10,000	1,550	11,550
3	15,000	3,205	18,205
4	20,000	5,525	25,525
5	25,000	8,577	33,577
10	50,000	37,655	87,655
15	75,000	99,746	174,746
20	100,000	215,008	315,008
25	125,000	415,903	540,903

Please note that the chart shows tax-free dollars. At the end of twenty-five years you would have added more than a half million dollars to your net worth by investing the money freed up by a company car. Only those unfamiliar with the power of regular savings multiplied by compound interest will be astonished at the cumulative total.

Even if you assume that without a second car it will cost you $1,000 a year for taxis and rented cars, and you invested only $4,000 each year for twenty-five years, at the end of that time you would still have added $432,727 to your net worth. The incredible fact is that owning an automobile is what prevents most of us from becoming financially independent. Remember my friend Richard who retired at fifty to devote himself to his golf game? Much of that retirement is being financed by the investments he made with the money saved by having a company car. The lesson could not be plainer: Get a company car, sell your present car, invest the savings, and be on your way to financial independence.

At-Home Entertainment Allowance

Inflation has produced many wrenching changes in the fabric of our society but perhaps none more serious than the appearance of the Bring-Your-Own-Bottle (BYOB) party. An evening of elegant dining and stimulating conversation has degenerated into a night of Fritos mashed into clam dip and fourteen simultaneous conversations about the excessive wage demands of cleaning ladies. A dinner party used to be something that people actually planned in advance, with due thought given to the menu, and wines selected to complement the meal. As we enter our second decade of inflation no one can afford to provide dinner and drinks to ten people any more, so thirty people are invited to bring their own drinks and partake of delicacies from Oscar Mayer. Even amid the furnishings of a $2,000-a-month apartment the prevailing aura is one of cheapness—a cheapness that affects the thought processes and conversation of the guests. Quentin Crisp observed this scene and wrote, "No party can be called a success until everyone is talking and no one is listening." In future years it may well be seen that the BYOB party marked the final stage in the decline of civilization as we know it.

Among those struggling to hold back the dark night are the 8.9 percent of corporations discovered by the American Management Association who permit their executives to charge the costs of home entertainment to their company. Perhaps with proper corporate funding the traditional dinner party can be restored to its rightful place as a preserver of tradition and as a stimulus for perceptive thought and analysis.

As a side benefit, if you can discharge a significant portion of your social obligations at company-paid, in-home dinners, you are, in effect, putting money into your pocket. In order to meet IRS requirements it is necessary that at each dinner or party a customer or someone with whom you do business be present. There also need be some discussion of a business nature, but it does not have to be extensive. A follow-up meeting can then wrap up your business affairs, after the party has created a mood of cordiality and friendship. In addition, the business guests you entertain at home will probably welcome the opportunity to meet new people and discuss matters of a nonbusiness nature.

If you are already authorized to entertain in restaurants, a trial run of an in-home dinner might be in order. Be sure to collect all the receipts for food, drinks, and other expenses so that the costs are fully documented. If the charges get past the auditing department, you will have a new way of socializing with your customers or clients, simultaneously reducing your home entertainment costs and assisting in the effort to restore grace and civility to the American social scene.

A Liberal Expense Account

In June of 1775, the Continental Congress offered George Washington the post of Commander-in-Chief of the Continental Armies at an annual salary of $25,000. At a time when a captain in the same army was paid $20 per month this was thought to be a princely sum. In reply, Washington wrote, "As to pay, sir, I beg leave to Assure the Congress that . . . no pecuniary consideration could have tempted me to have accepted this arduous employment. . . . I do not wish to make a Profit from it. I will keep an exact account of my expences (sic). Those I doubt not they will discharge, and that is all I desire." *

---

* *George Washington's Expense Account* by Marvin Kitman, Simon & Schuster, New York, 1970

The Congress greeted that suggestion with cries of joy and the Father of Our Country was widely praised for his patriotic generosity. Eight years later, upon the successful conclusion of the war, General Washington submitted his first, and final, expense account, which totalled out to $449,261.51. One can assume that the document was greeted with somewhat less enthusiasm than the general's first letter on the subject.

Every perks player is in the debt of General Washington, who forever set the style and the standard for compiling expense accounts, and to Marvin Kitman whose prodigious research made General Washington's ledgers available for the enlightenment of all. Kitman points out that, early on. General Washington established the seven basic principles of expense accounting:

1. Each account should be greater than the one before; start small and grow gradually.
2. Omit nothing.
3. Add everything possible.
4. On small expenses, be specific. On large expenses be vague.
5. Intermingle personal and business expenses.
6. Always pick up the check for associates.
7. Know what the traffic will bear.

General Washington had a finely developed sense of the perks that were due him. The army may have suffered through the winter at Valley Forge but the general preferred the bright lights of Philadelphia, where his prowess on the dance floor left the ladies gasping in admiration. A quick day-trip to Valley Forge, northwest of the city, usually brought the general back to his quarters in time for the evening meal. General Washington was proud of the table he set, and guests came away impressed by the linen tablecloths, the gleaming silver, and the fine cuisine. Many were also impressed by the quantity of alcohol consumed. One visitor wrote in his diary, "Given cider and punch for lunch; rum and brandy before dinner; Madeira, port and sherry at dinner; punch and liqueurs with the ladies; and wine, spirit and punch till bedtime, all in punch bowls big enough to swim in.''

General Washington was also generous with the lower classes; in Boston, he tipped a chambermaid $25 (approximately $250 in today's money). On the record, one must infer that the service today in Boston's hotels is not what it used to be. The smallest item in the ledger is dated March 28, 1776, "To Mr. Jos. Stanbury, cut glass vinegar cruets and salt cellars, $20.80." Note that the item is recorded to the penny, which is a sound principle of expense accounting that the general did not always follow. The monthly charges for unspecified household expenses began at $1,000, rose to $2,000 in 1778, $3,000 in 1779, and after 1780 held steady at $5,000. Rounding off to even dollars is never to be recommended, unless one is of the stature of the general.

When General Washington submitted his accounts, he apologized for the lack of supporting receipts, but tactfully pointed out that there had been a war on. Ever eager to be helpful, he included a summary:

Household Expences (sic)	157,330.64	
Secret Intelligence	62,762.00	
Travel Expenses	81,490.93	
Miscellaneous	117,222.62	
Total	414,108.21	(Actually 418,806.19)
Interest	7,488.00	
Expences (sic) of Mrs. W.	27,665.30	
	449,261.51	

The cool daring of a man who could list almost 25 percent of his expenses as "Miscellaneous" was obviously an essential element in winning the war. Also essential was the comforting embrace of his wife, and the $27K that it cost the Congress was a small price to pay for the maintenance of the general's morale. Fortunately for the Congressional budget, the general's wife was considerably older than he, and acknowledged to be one of the plainest women in The Colonies, and the general did not require her solace more than once or twice a year during the course of the conflict.

When General Washington was eventually elected our first president he offered Congress the same financial arrangement under which he had led their army to victory. They declined with thanks, and the general had to accept a straight salary. It was Congress's first, and perhaps most successful, attempt to control federal expenditures.

Learn from our revered first president: If you don't now have a company expense account, get one as soon as possible. You may be in the wrong job or you may be too low on the corporate organization chart or you may be at the right level but in the wrong position or you may work for the wrong company. Whatever the reason, you should be working to correct your plight. Without a liberal expense account, the cost of your social life will be a daunting burden. Dinner for two in almost any big city restaurant these days is going to cost you $50 or more, unless you eschew wine in favor of the house aqua pura. An evening with your spouse in which the two of you automatically look for the cheapest item on the menu inevitably loses much of its enchantment. It also takes a sturdy psyche to withstand the scornful look of the waiter as you order two servings of Salisbury steak and no wine, please. Wouldn't you rather be dining at Le Gourmet with the great and the near-great, seeing and being seen? Get promoted; take a transfer to another position; go with another company—do whatever it takes, but get yourself an expense account. Get with it— no one pays for restaurant meals with his own money anymore! Your boss doesn't do it, his boss doesn't do it, and there's no reason for you to do it! Think of it; you join the "I'll buy your lunch today and you buy mine tomorrow" crowd and suddenly your daily expenses go down and you begin to associate with the movers and shakers of the business world. All you need is a few friends on expense accounts and you need never pay for your own lunch again.

You buy theirs and they buy yours. It's the American way!

An expense account also offers other opportunities for cash savings and enhanced image creation. Are you a sports fan? Do you enjoy watching oddly dressed hooligans pummeling one another about an ice rink while drunks in the stands curse one another and spill beer on you in high glee? Or do you fancy a tasteful afternoon surrounded by elegantly attired patricians watching lithesome lads and lassies in short trousers hitting topspin forehands while you murmur appreciatively, "Well played." Whatever your sporting interests, there is no reason for you to continue to bear the heavy cost of pursuing them. Your company will assist in reducing your out-of-pocket expenses; all that is required is that you find a client or customer of like interest and have him join you in your play. The two of you can have a ripping time vicariously reliving your school days when your feet had wings and your hands were unerring in their sureness. You return home, exhilarated by exposure to your favorite sport, gratified that the company paid for your outing, and heartened by the increased rapport with your business associate. What could be more perfect?

A sporting event is also a smashing place in which to meet members of the opposite sex. The informality of the occasion and the general milling about provide almost unlimited opportunities for casual introductory remarks. In addition, you can select the socioeconomic level in which you wish to mingle by the choice of sport. If your preference runs to the rough-and-tumble world of the working class, bowling tournaments and wrestling matches offer unparalleled occasions for social encounters with persons who approach life in direct, realistic terms. Attendance at a golf tournament puts you in touch with the country club set. Do not take a seat in one of the temporary bleachers erected for the event; only fanatical golfing enthusiasts will sit all day waiting for a glimpse of their favorite players, and those kinds of fans are almost always hopelessly inept socially. The wisest course is to stroll the fairways, moving from one gallery to another and allowing fortune to throw opportunities your way.

A polo match is an excellent opportunity to meet the horsey set. The match will last most of the afternoon, with frequent rest periods offering maximum chances for social interaction. If you know little of polo, do not pretend otherwise; even the most ingenuous charmer who catches your eye will have a full knowledge of the game and its history. Be prepared to discuss the differences between the American and Argentinean styles of attack and the proper conformation of a good pony, with special reference to the need for sturdy hocks. If your knowledge is limited, say so and ask for guidance. You will be treated to a two-hour monologue on the sport and it will be difficult to steer the conversation into more promising areas, but if you are patient, eventually you can reach the serious question of having dinner together that evening (on the company expense account, of course). Your biggest problem will be the automobile you arrived in, the only Chevy in sight. If you are going to mingle with the horsey set, you will have to act the part. Be prepared to play the game all the way or not at all.

The following are some activities you should not consider if your purpose is to meet new people or improve your social contacts.

YACHT RACES

Everyone is in one of two places, the bar of the sponsoring yacht club or on a boat watching the start of the race. Those in the bar will either be other social climbers or the yacht club members who have been professional drunks since FDR drove them to it in 1936. Eventually, all those on the boats will return to the club, but yachting people already know everyone they care to know and your efforts to engage them in conversation will be greeted by stony silence.

BASEBALL OR FOOTBALL GAMES

The fixed seats and narrow aisles prevent much mingling except at the refreshment stands where the fierce struggle for space at the counter precludes any speech other than grunts and curses. There is considerable traffic in the aisles, but it consists mainly of vandals on their worst behavior. The people in the seats around you will be either too engrossed in the game or their flasks of whiskey to pay attention to you.

PROFESSIONAL SOCCER

The matches themselves are actually wonderful places to meet people because the fans are enthusiastic and cheerful and happily converse with everyone around them. The difficulty is that no one speaks English and unless you have a working acquaintance with either Spanish, Italian, or Greek you will be at a disadvantage.

If your interests are more intellectual, two tickets to the opera or ballet will add a soupçon of culture to your expense account and may intimidate an auditor into searching elsewhere for his prey. If your interests are less esoteric, most massage parlors now accept credit cards—although any "extra services" provided by your masseuse should be paid in cash. In consideration of their corporate clients, few massage parlors use names on the charge slip that might cause complications with the auditing department. Names like *The Hideaway* or *Tower East* connote an impression of a quiet little restaurant where you and a client discussed matters of import to your company.

It is helpful to have a collection of restaurant receipts to use when filling out your expense account, and many managers routinely tear off the stubs from restaurant bills. Should you feel this maneuver detracts from your image as a person of consequence, you may obtain 100 blank restaurant receipts in fifty styles from D & K Sales, P.O. Box 82, Kempton, PA 19529. The cost is $5.98, and satisfaction is guaranteed.

An expense account can also help provide some of the vestments needed to maintain your image as an executive on a fast track. I first learned this a few years ago while

131

attending a professional convention in St. Louis. While wandering about the exhibits I encountered Mike, an old friend, and arm in arm we left the convention hall to seek a restaurant for a luncheon reunion. At the close of the meal I grandly offered to pick up the check as a demonstration of the heights to which I had risen in the world. Mike blandly allowed me to do so with none of the usual insincere protests. While walking back to the convention hall we passed a men's haberdashery and Mike detoured into it to purchase two rather elegant shirts and a tie. I noticed that he charged the items with his company credit card and asked, "Doesn't it get rather complicated separating your personal expenses from business expenses when you make out your expense account?"

I received a look much favored by my third-grade teacher as Mike replied, "What personal? It's all business."

Giving new meaning to the word obtuse, I persisted, "But how can a shirt be a business expense?"

"It's not a shirt on the expense account, dummy; it's the lunch we just had."

"But this isn't a restaurant," I remarked with what I considered to be unassailable logic.

"Nooo shit!" Mike responded as he patted me on the back approvingly. "Look," he said as he showed me the charge slip. The merchant establishment was shown on the slip as "Arnie's"; there was no indication of what Arnie purveyed to the public. "As far as the accounting department knows," Mike explained, "Arnie's is a restaurant."

Mike went on to reveal how most of his wardrobe was charged to out-of-town's men's shops in lieu of meals. Lunch for two provided $25 to $30 worth of apparel, and dinner for two financed $50 to $60 worth. Occasionally, a dinner for six provided the wherewithal for a suit, but Mike never claimed that amount more than two or three times a year. The end result was that Mike dressed as well as most company presidents, which may have had something to do with his becoming a vice-president by the age of 35. Or perhaps it was his enterprising spirit.

In every city there are clothing shops for men and women whose names do not indicate that they sell apparel and are sought out by knowing users of company credit cards. In New York we have shops for men—Arthur's Court, Ponte Vecchio, Votano—and shops for women—Tahari's, Cazou, Entin—where items of apparel can be purchased with minimum risk that a sharp-eyed auditor will know that the establishment is not a restaurant or bar. The safest course is to patronize out-of-town establishments where the true identity of the shop is unlikely to be known to the auditors back in the home office.

The only cloud on the expense account horizon is a proposal in the Senate that would permit only one-half the cost of business meals to be deducted by the company. The apparent assumption is that the corporate employee would be buying his own lunch were it not for the presence of the customer; therefore, the company should only be allowed to deduct the cost of the customer's meal. This proposal met with forceful opposition by the restaurant worker's union, and Senator Dole agreed to drop the idea if the restaurant workers will agree to a plan to more accurately account for tips on their tax returns. The restaurant workers are aghast at that suggestion, and the matter is now at a standoff.

We recall a similar effort by Jimmy Carter to do away with the "three martini lunch." I was never certain with whom Jimmy had been associating, because my experience is that the only people who take three martinis at lunchtime are actors who immediately head home for a long nap before the evening performance. Either the business folk in Plains have an inordinate fondness for midday martinis or Jimmy broke bread each noon with itinerant acting troupes passing through town. We must hope that Senator Dole's proposal meets the same fate as the suggestion of our former president, a long period of neglect followed by a decent burial.

Comprehensive Medical Plans

Your company already has a medical plan that provides extensive coverage for you and all the other employees, right? So how can this be a perk if everyone has it? Ah, but everyone doesn't have it to the same degree. I would be willing to bet that the CEO of your company has no deductible on his medical coverage as you do and that there are no limits on his coverage for payments in any one year or a lifetime. He is also probably covered for routine visits by him and his family to the family doctor and for the costs of prescriptions. He may even be covered for the cost of eyeglasses and hearing aids, if necessary. He is undoubtedly covered for psychiatric care on an out-patient or institutional basis. Your CEO and his family are also likely to be covered for complete dental expenses, which in a home with 2.4 children can be a considerable portion of the family budget.

The AMA survey found that 75.6 percent of the surveyed companies reported a comprehensive medical plan for at least one level of management. In some cases coverage was provided by adding on to the company's existing medical plan while in others the executive was simply reimbursed for all expenses not covered by the company plan. The extra costs per executive averaged $1,668 annually, which represents $3,000 or more dollars of pretax income savings for the executives involved. The average participation for all industries showed 46.9 percent providing the coverage to CEOs and 28.7 percent to middle managers.

Are you among the 28.7 percent of middle managers whose company values their services so highly that they are willing to provide this profitable little perk? If not, it might be a suitable topic for discussion at your next salary review. You probably aren't going to get all the salary increase you hope for and are probably entitled to, and a request for additional medical or dental coverage might receive a favorable hearing.

— 9 —

Living the Good Life

In one of his notebooks Samuel Butler once wrote, "All of the animals excepting man know that the principal business of life is to enjoy it." Dedicated players in the Perks Game have set themselves the task of refuting Butler's observation and, as the fellow who applies the body makeup at the Folies Bérgère remarked, "It's a dirty, nasty business, but somebody's got to do it." With that in mind let's look at some of the ways in which a perks player can enjoy a few of the things in life that make it more enjoyable.

Club Memberships

Those of us weaned on John O'Hara and F. Scott Fitzgerald have never gotten over the impression that "the rich are very different from you and me." For me the symbol of real wealth was never an imposing mansion because at an early age I realized that any bootlegger could build a palace. In my youth, through a series of occurrences too convoluted to describe here, I spent much of one summer bowling and shooting pool in the basement of an English Tudor mansion that occupied one-half square block in the finest section of River Forest, then, and perhaps now, Chicago's most expensive suburb. Aside from the entertainment facilities and the lavish furnishings of the palazzo, I was most impressed with an upstairs bathroom that had a tub carved out of onyx, and what appeared to be solid gold faucets. Adjoining the main building was a two-story garage containing a small fleet of powerful sedans, with servants quarters above. The immaculate lawns and towering oaks and elms were entirely surrounded by a stout fence of cast iron higher than one could reach. The only discordant note was the perpetual presence across the street of two FBI agents in an automobile who photographed each guest upon arrival and departure. My host, the owner of this formidable estate, was one Anthony Accardo, a man of few words and gracious hospitality, known to the readers of the Chicago *Herald-Examiner* as Tony (Big Tuna) Accardo, the reputed head of the Syndicate. This was puzzling to the neighbors, who owned that the Accardo family was among the most quiet and decorous of the citizens of River Forest. At that time, the terms Mafia and Cosa Nostra were unknown to Chicagoans and would have been little understood. In Chicago we took pride in a Syndicate which embraced all nationalities and both political parties. As the alleged head of this enterprise Mr. Accardo was accorded the respect given any successful businessman, and when he and his family went on a tour of Europe, the Chicago Police Department sent along a lieutenant to secure cigarettes, coffee, and sweet rolls when needed and to ensure that no untoward incident marred the tranquil passage of the Accardos through the capitals of Europe. When Mr. Accardo's son was married in a stunningly impressive ceremony in the most fashionable Catholic Church in River Forest, the church overflowed with notables of public and private life, and the statement was made that the next city and county budgets were decided upon at the reception.

Mr. Accardo's partner, Paul (The Waiter) Ricca had an establishment only slightly less imposing three blocks further north on Franklin Avenue, and a host of Mr. Accardo's business associates, including many captains in the police force, numerous aldermen, several municipal judges, county assessors, and high officials of the Chicago Sanitary District, had residences almost as impressive as the Accardo domicile. Given all that, one can understand my feeling that a mansion was not a sign of true wealth.

My vision of real money came the day I pedalled my bicycle west on Lake Street through the working-class suburbs of Northlake and Melrose Park and out into what was then open country and suddenly came upon a golf course. But not just a golf course, rather an expanse of trees and greenery so properly proportioned and perfectly manicured that I could only gaze in awe. Medinah Country Club could have inspired George S. Kaufman's remark when he saw Moss Hart's estate in Bucks County: "It just shows what God could have done if He'd only had the money." Three long fairways with matching sculptured greens were visible from my vantage point; I was staggered to see only one foursome on that expanse. It seemed to my wondering eyes that those three fairways alone could have encompassed all nine holes of the Columbus Park Golf Course where I was then diligently learning the game at a punishing price of fifty cents per round. As the foursome approached I saw that only two carried clubs while two others strode along in blitheful unawareness of the splendor surrounding them. The group stopped and one member was handed a club while he gazed thoughtfully toward the green. I realized that I was seeing not a foursome but a twosome accompanied by caddies, legendary figures of whom I had heard but had never seen. I was certain that to be a caddy at the Medinah Country Club one needed to be almost as rich as the members, for who but the scions of the wealthy was fit to carry a full set of brand-new Walter Hagen woods and irons and would never hesitate to offer an untouched Titleist at even the most threatening water hole? I experienced a sensation best expressed many years later in the movie *Diner*, in which two youths from a working-class neighborhood see a girl ride past on a handsome horse on the far side of a white fence marking the boundaries of a country estate. One turns to the other and says, "Ever get the feelin' there's somethin' goin' on we don't know nothin' about?"

Since that day the private country club has served as my symbol of the wealth and status to which we all presumably strive. Of course, there are country clubs and country clubs. The variations are as wide as the fairway on a driving range and as deep as the bunkers at Pinehurst. There is little satisfaction in belonging to a club with hundreds of members pulling caddy carts behind them and drinking cans of Schlitz as they mill about at each tee waiting their turn. Unfortunately, for most of us, that is the only type of club we can afford and as Groucho Marx once observed, "I wouldn't want to belong to a club that would have me as a member." The real satisfaction comes from membership in a club where a respectful caddy follows each player as he strides down a fairway into which weeds dare not venture, where the preferred libation in the clubhouse is a Tanqueray martini, very dry, where the conversation revolves around the latest sail design for three-meter sloops and where each Saturday night, candlelight dinner dances are attended by men and women for whom being overweight is an unfortunate condition of the working poor.

Even if we had the money, we probably couldn't get in. The membership committee screens applicants carefully to weed out the eager but bumptious climber anxious to socialize with his betters. ("Good grief. The man is likely to begin selling me insurance in the locker room. He won't do, simply won't do.") Applicants may find neighbors and acquaintances being questioned as to their fitness for membership at Elysian Knolls. ("I'm sorry to report that although he seems a decent chap his wife wears a size 13 and his children are fond of doing cannonballs off the diving board at the community pool.") Sorrowful murmurs of, "Too awful," and "Good heavens!" are heard as the black balls cascade into the bowl. The reality for most of us is that the country club life of the truly wealthy can only be known through books or movies.

Nevertheless, at a step below the playing fields of the very rich lie hundreds of country clubs where life is infinitely more gracious and enjoyable than a season membership at Bethpage State Park or Waveland Golf Course. A company-sponsored membership in a good country club offers entrée to a world of comfort and relaxation that, if not quite up to the standards of Medinah or Winged Foot, is still a welcome relief from the drab surroundings of everyday life.

The two great advantages of a corporate membership are that you don't have to pay for it and you don't have to pass muster by the membership committee, either qualification sufficient to knock most of us out of the box. The two parties usually have an understanding that the club will accept all those named by the corporation and the company will not name someone obviously unfit. In order to fulfill their part of the bargain many companies have a range of club memberships to bestow on deserving employees. At the basic level, a division sales manager might have to be content with a club where the Saturday night dinner dance has the ambiance of a sock-hop at the local high school, with men in polo shirts and slacks and women in (ugh!) designer jeans careening about the dance floor to cha-cha records played by the teenage son of the club president. Dinner will be Chicken Kiev and petits pois both recently thawed and served by teenage girls and accompanied by vintage Almaden. After midnight there will be a smidgin of groping as dance partners are exchanged, but by one A.M. everyone will be headed for the parking lot to get the babysitter home.

A vice president might find at his club that sport coats are acceptable attire on Saturday night, but his wife will feel that she should have a new dress once in awhile to stave off the stares of the ruling clique. The band is likely to be a quartet of students from the local junior college under strict orders not to play any of that "freaky" music. Dinner will be served by elderly ladies in starched white aprons and consist of prime ribs and baked potato, and the dessert will have rum in it. Wine will be a choice of Italian white or French red and the wives of some of the older members will drink more than they can handle. The dancing will be taken quite seriously and switching of partners will be commonplace. By three A.M. everyone will have left except some of the unmarried club members and those whose children are away at school, who will be gathered together, boozily recalling the exact words to six verses of their college song.

The CEO will find it necessary at his club to dress for Saturday night, and his wife will be expected to spare the others the sight of the same gown more than twice a year. There will be candles and flowers on each table, and few will leave to chance whom their tablemates will be. Dinner will be served by dark-clad waiters; veal piccata will be a popular favorite, with two vegetables and never the appearance of a potato. Dessert will be raspberries in whipped cream laced with Grand Marnier; many of those dining will have cognac as an accompaniment. The wines will all be French, and there will be much discussion of vintages and bouquet and body, and tales will be told of visits to the most marvelous little villages in Normandy where the most incredible wine is served that isn't even exported to the States. The orchestra will be professional in appearance if not in ability and the CEO and wife should know all variations on the two-step and also have a nodding acquaintance with disco moves to demonstrate the retention of their youthful spirit. If necessary, both may have to trim down so that they no longer need patronize the Stylishly Stout departments at Bloomingdale's. By two A.M. the parking lot will be empty, the flagging energy level of the club members long since forcing them home to bed.

The AMA found that 61 percent of the companies responding to their survey reported paid memberships in various types of clubs, and almost 5 percent said that they extended the privilege to middle managers. Do not infer from this that credit and collection managers are to be found among the members at Medinah or Baltusrol or Burlingame. If there are corporate members at those or similar clubs, we can rest assured that it is either the president or chairman of the board, and that the company is in the Fortune 500 group.

The type of club to which most of us will belong through our company's largesse is probably a modest little retreat with too many members and too few groundskeepers. There is however one way in which an occasional glimpse can be had of life at the top. Most clubs, even the most exclusive, extend guest privileges to members from other private clubs, even the least distinguished, who are visiting from elsewhere. All that is required is a phone call a day in advance to make sure that the annual Members' Day Tournament or something of the sort is not being held and you will be accorded the privilege of inhaling the aroma of true wealth and status, even if it is only for an afternoon. Be prepared to pay handsomely for the privilege. At many exclusive clubs a round of golf for a guest costs $50, and that does not include the caddy fee or tips to the locker room attendant and the fellow in the pro shop who cleans your clubs. Casual attire, so long as it is not jeans, will cause no raised eyebrows at lunch or while having drinks in the bar, but if you plan on dinner, a change of clothes will be necessary. It is best to avoid the card games in the men's locker room. The chips will not represent nickels, dimes, and quarters but rather fives, tens, and fifties. Backgammon is now a popular country club pastime whose wagering level is usually within reason: Games at $5 each can while away a pleasant hour or so without costing more than $50 or $100. Watch out for the doubling cube; it can quickly turn a $5 game into a $40 game in only three turns. Do not expect to be invited to the dance in the evening; hospitality does have its limits. In addition, a friend can be included on your guest pass if he is also a member of a club, and you will both need your club membership cards to establish your bona fides.

Resort Facilities and Yachts

Ah, for the days when the Robber Barons of America vied with one another for the size and appointments of their sea-going offices. No tycoon was content until he had a mansion in Newport and a yacht tied to the dock. J. P.

Morgan's *Corsair* was the most famous of the fleet, and hardened corporate directors could be reduced to school-girlish incoherency by an invitation to sail the Greek Isles with the master financier. Now that Aristotle Onassis has gone to his reward and the *Christina* is in drydock, about all that is left is the yacht of movie mogul Sam Speigel, whose first screen credits listed him as S. P. Eagle and who cannot resist the old impulse to make a buck; he rents out the yacht to other film makers needing an impressive nautical backdrop for a Harold Robbins or Sidney Sheldon screenplay.

There is one bright spot in this gloomy picture: businessmen from Asia. The Japanese have so far managed to control their need for sailing vessels, but a number of entrepreneurs from Hong Kong and Singapore find a yacht an indispensable tool of their trade and it is to be hoped the Japanese will soon follow suit. Perhaps even Merrill Lynch will succumb to the call of the sea now they have formed a partnership with Fung King Hey, Hong Kong's leading financial wizard. Messrs Fung and Merrill Lynch are buying into one another's businesses and the outcome will leave Mr. Fung as Merrill Lynch's major stockholder. Mr. Fung maintains a luxurious yacht, *Bo-Bo,* meaning "Beloved One" and named after his wife, and much of Mr. Fung's business affairs are conducted from the sun deck of his yacht after he has swum his daily ten laps around the vessel. The ability of a yacht to affect the thinking processes of those aboard is underscored by the fact that Merrill Lynch paid 50 percent over the market price for the shares they purchased in Mr. Fung's various enterprises. Given Mr. Fung's ability to create wealth, the shares were probably a bargain: Fung arrived in Hong Kong in 1948 with nothing and now has a personal fortune estimated at $300 million.

Alas and alack, however, the great days of American corporate yachting appear to be over. Only 2.3 percent of the companies responding to the AMA survey indicated that they provided a yacht on which their executives could conduct their business. And worst of all, of that group, more than one-third charge the executives on a daily basis if the yacht is used for personal enjoyment. I mean, how cheap can you get?

The prevalance of company-owned resort facilities is in even more serious decline. Only 1.9 percent of the companies reported the availability of a company-owned resort. Although the report doesn't say so, my impression is that most are hunting or shooting lodges and quite a few are located in Canada. A company jet almost always accompanies the corporate resort; how else can you get to the damn place? Again, more than half the companies ask their executives to pay for their own food or else charge them a per diem rate while using the facility. I mean, I'm talking *cheap!*

If a sojourn at sea is your object, the most feasible course is to establish an affiliation with an Asian businessman or a movie manipulator, expecting that occasionally you will spend some time aboard his yacht discussing business. The best way to experience the thrill of a private hunting preserve is to buddy up to a titled Englishman whose family still owns a thousand or so acres of heather and brae in Scotland and hope to be included in next year's grouse shooting. If this comes about, remember the grouse are the small birds erupting from the gorse and not the oddly dressed natives beating sticks together and advancing across the field. And don't forget your woolies; the laird's "wee hoose" will be four stories of solid stone with a chill in each room sufficient to hang meat, and a peat fire providing no more warmth than the exhaust from a well-played bagpipe.

Overseas Travel

It's the rare company today that doesn't have some kind of overseas operation even if it's just a sales office. If the vast potential of overseas markets is ever to be properly exploited by your company, it will require the attention of various executives from corporate headquarters. There is no reason why you should not be in the group bringing the benefits of American know-how to your overseas operation. Obviously, your CEO is going to have first call on overseas junkets, at least on those with Paris, London, or Geneva as their destination. Vice presidents will settle for Rome, Brussels, and Stockholm. You may have to be content with Stuttgart, Palermo, and Addis Ababa, but a trip is a trip. Who knows, even in Palermo you may run into a movie biggie or an English lord who, if far enough into his cups, might extend an invitation to a yachting cruise or a weekend at the family estate in the Cotswolds.

In any event, travel is beneficial, no matter what the destination. It gets you out of the office and into new places and, most important of all, gives you some devastating ploys at business and social gatherings. Here is where your out-of-the-way bourne comes in handy: "I was much impressed with the entrepreneurial spirit I found in Abidjan and would think that the socialist opposition will find it sticky going. I am recommending that we substantially increase our investment there." That ploy accomplishes a number of things. First, it establishes you as a world traveler, essential in the era of multinational corporations. Second, it implies that you are in a position to make a formal study of a nation's economic system. Third, it enhances your image as a person of import whose investment recommendations are weighty enough to cause flurries of activity on the Paris Bourse. Best of all, hardly anyone will know where Abidjan is let alone be able to challenge your statement. Should an ingenuous person inquire as to the location of Abidjan, restrict your answer to, "Capital of the Ivory Coast. Fascinating country, simply fascinating."

If you are so unfortunate as to be sent to the well-traveled capitals of Europe, there is little you can say that hasn't already been said a thousand times over. The safest course is to say nothing other than to indicate you just returned from three weeks on the Continent. Treat the event with casual nonchalance, implying that you know that everyone else has been there so often it's not worth discussing.

What to do if your efforts to promote visits to your European agents or offices prove unsuccessful? A friend of mine was faced with that problem some years ago. Fred was a product manager responsible for the marketing of polyethylene film and yearned for overseas travel. The company did considerable business in Europe but the vice president of marketing, to whom Fred reported, monopolized all visits to their European distributors. All of Fred's efforts to promote a trip to Europe for himself were rebuffed because, as Fred eventually discovered, his boss had a lady friend in Rotterdam who required frequent demonstrations of affection. Fred shifted tactics and looked across the Pacific to Australia, reasoning that if he could establish a market for his products Down Under, his boss would not be able to take the time to personally oversee the business. (Even a turnaround trip to Australia takes three days, which would have to come out of the time the boss devoted to his duties in Rotterdam.)

Without saying anything to his boss, Fred contacted the Australian consul and the Australian Trade Commission and obtained a list of possible buyers of his polyethylene film. After considerable correspondence Fred approached his boss with letters of interest from a number of firms in Australia and asked permission to send them samples of the various types of polyethylene film. Fred's boss, enervated from a debilitating four days in Rotterdam and a long flight home, approved the project with little thought. In a relatively short while Fred was generating close to half a million dollars in sales to Australia, and he soon began making semiannual visits there.

Over the next few years Fred's sales to Australia and New Zealand progressed smartly and Fred's wanderlust was partially satisfied by his visits to the antipodes with stopovers in Tahiti, Fiji, and Hawaii. Shortly thereafter the president of Fred's company decided that the Japanese market could no longer be ignored and inquired as to what was being done in the Far East. Fred's boss could only point to their modest effort in Australia as evidence of involvement in that area. The president quickly chartered Fred to begin looking into how best to sell their wares in Japan. Three years later Fred was in charge of his company's Far East operations and directing a small staff out of a suite of offices in San Francisco. Today he is still there, contentedly shuttling between Tokyo, Singapore, Jakarta, Melbourne, Manila, and Christchurch, and earning as much as his old boss.

Even if you cannot establish an overseas operation of your own, you may be able to travel to trade shows and conventions held in other countries. European and Asian cities vie with one another to sponsor events that will lure American businessmen to their city gates. The location need not be particularly desirable and in fact probably won't be; the Riviera or the Costa del Sol don't have to work hard at attracting visitors. That's why you have a monster trade fair in Leipzig, the largest book fair in Frankfurt, and a giant packaging exposition in Dusseldorf. Almost every industry has some sort of fair, convention, or exposition held annually or biennially in either Europe or Asia. It's time you disabused yourself of the notion that your presence is not an absolute requirement at the trade show for your industry. If nothing else, perhaps you can wangle passage as aide de camp for your boss. Let him know you will be happy to take on onerous little chores such as handling all those boring travel arrangements or collecting brochures on promising equipment and techniques at the exhibit hall. Reassure him that your presence will allow him to focus his energies on the essential person-to-person contacts so beneficial to the company and that his evenings will be entirely his own since you will be found nightly in the town library pursuing your lifetime interest in the early history of the Hanseatic League.

A nice feature of most trade shows is the gracious hospitality of exhibitors. It requires extreme misanthropy for a visitor to pay for a meal or buy a drink at a trade fair. There is, however, no requirement that you forgo appending those meals or drinks to your expense account. After all, the company expects to pay for those necessities, and to not include them in your accounting of the trip is to set an undesirable precedent for those who will follow. Exhibitors are also eager for possible buyers to visit their offices and manufacturing facilities, there to be suitably impressed with the quality and price of the goods. Many publishing executives spend the second week of each October at the Frankfurt Book Fair and then ten days or so touring northern Italy to observe the wonders of Italian four-color printing plants. There must be extensive annual changes in color printing technology since a yearly visit is thought essential by many publishing company executives. This has become such a ritual that after some years of observance, the printing plant workers in Milan have come to know American vice presidents almost as well as their own foremen.

Every two years Dusseldorf sponsors Interpak, an international exposition of food processing and packaging equipment, primarily for the confectionary industry. Candy makers from all over the world descend on the Ruhr for a week in May to sample the local Riesling and examine the latest in candy-making technology. Since no prudent businessman would commit to purchasing equipment from nothing more than a demonstration at a trade show, visits to users of the equipment are necessary so that the equipment can be seen in actual operation. There are many suppliers, and users are distributed from Malmo to Messina, from Aldershot to Athens. The European manufacturers recognize their obligations and are happy to pay for the travel costs of their friends from across the Atlantic. Each manufacturer assumes the travel costs of a visitor from his last stop to the user location specified by the manufacturer. From there he is passed on to the next manufacturer for the next stop in his Grand Tour. The highlight of most tours is a leisurely sail down the Rhine with a stop in each major city to savor the local ambiance and watch the candy machines in operation. An American candy maker who plans his itinerary properly can visit over the course of a few years all the essential tourist areas of Europe at no personal cost.

The principal peril to those attending Interpak was removed a few years ago when Cesare M. retired. Cesare was a senior executive with a food equipment manufacturer in Milan and each year extended an invitation to a select group of American candy makers to join him in a tour of the factories using Cesare's equipment. Rather than using the impersonal service of a limousine, Cesare personally chauffeured his guests in the latest model Porsche. Those who were there still tell of the experience of watching Cesare hurtling down the Autostrade at 120 MPH and forcing other cars to give way while gesturing with both hands as he turned his head to talk to his passengers. It should be noted that Cesare was entirely in the right, since in Italy right of way is determined by engine displacement. To the uninitiated, one of the memorable sights of their life is to be in the left lane on an Italian highway and see a small dot in the rear view mirror suddenly grow larger and larger at alarming speed. Before the mind can adjust, a Maserati or Mercedes fills your mirror, the front bumper six inches from your tailpipe, and the sound of a powerful horn fills your head as the driver behind indignantly has to slow down. With shaking hands you begin to pull over into the right hand lane and with an angry roar the other car swerves by while you are still halfway in the left lane, missing your fender by inches. After that, you leave the left lane to the mighty.

First-class Air Travel

For many executives the bitterest pill of the current recession is the loss of first-class air privileges. To step into the economy section of a coast-to-coast flight and see dozens of immaculately garbed senior executives cheek by jowl with guitar-toting teenagers, salesmen in polyester suits, old ladies fumbling with their seat belts, and hordes of squalling infants, all being served tiny portions of inedible foodstuffs by harried stewardesses is enough to bring tears to one's eyes. The pathetic attempts of the executives to insulate themselves from their surroundings by plunging into the paperwork in their briefcases only makes the scene more poignant. Few in first class can repress a shudder as the aisle curtain is mercifully drawn, shutting off the depressing view astern. "There but for the grace of my CEO go I" is the unspoken thought that ripples through first class like a communal shiver at a horror movie.

The gravity of the situation is illustrated by the AMA survey, which found that only 43.6 percent of the companies responding normally provide first-class air travel for even one level of management. About half the other companies will permit first-class travel under various conditions, usually if no coach seats are available or if the flight is more than four hours. Fourteen companies reported that they never allow their executives to fly first class under any conditions.

The situation for middle managers is even more abysmal. Only 6.5 percent of the companies allow middle managers to travel first class, with a range from 8.8 percent in the insurance industry down to zero among utilities and transportation companies. For some reason, insurance companies fare best in this matter, with almost 60 percent of their CEOs allowed the pleasures of first class, 44 percent of their corporate officers, and 23 percent of their top management. Cut those figures in half and you have the scorecard for utilities and transportation companies. A sorrier picture of the precipitous decline in the quality of life could hardly be found.

An executive's only recourse is to carefully examine his company's travel policy to determine whether there are any loopholes that might be used to advantage. The most obvious possibility is where first-class travel is permitted if there are no other seats available; this was discussed in an earlier chapter in some detail. Given the restrictive travel policies of most companies today, however, the outlook is not bright. I can offer one stratagem that can alleviate if not correct the problem. On many flights the aircraft will have not two but three classes of seating: first class, economy, and a business-class section referred to as "Ambassador Class" or by some other fancy title. The business section is usually only found on the widebody jets and will have eight seats across instead of the six found in first class or the ten in coach. If you wait and board the plane last, you can usually spot a vacant seat or two in the business section and, if you occupy one, will seldom be challenged. If a last-minute passenger does show up with a boarding pass for the seat, you simply excuse it as an error and take another seat in the section. The worst that can happen is you have to take your original seat back in steerage. Unlike first class, where the flight attendant matches names against a roster, in business class no attendant will question your right to the seat. Relax and enjoy the free champagne, a meal that if not haute cuisine is at least edible, a free movie, and the comfort of a wider seat with more leg room. Best of all, you will be among your own kind, with the sounds of gum-snapping, the wails of children, the snappish retorts of overworked attendants, and the jokes of the Dacron crowd far behind.

If there is no business-class section on a flight and there is no way you can bend the company rules to get a first-class seat, you are going to have to make the best of it. If at all possible, avoid eating the meal served on the plane; have lunch or dinner in a decent restaurant either before or after the flight. While the others are searching through their trays for a trace of food flavor, you can relax with a couple of small bottles of the airline's California wine, which is usually quite good. If the meal cannot be avoided, order from the special menus the airlines have available. Even if you're not a vegetarian or don't have special dietetic requirements, you're better off with one of those selections than with the regular meal. Many airlines offer a sandwich plate that is often rather tasty. There is one special meal offered by American and TWA that is outstanding: the seafood platter. The special meals must be ordered at least twenty-four hours in advance of the flight. Do not depend on the attendant to find you with your special meal; unless you identify yourself when boarding, someone else will get it, probably a crew member in whom the attendant has a special interest.

While ordering your special meal you can also obtain preassigned seats, for both the outgoing and the return flights. In order to secure your seat you must obtain your boarding pass at least thirty minutes before the flight is scheduled to depart. If you arrive after that, you are likely to find that your seat has been assigned to someone else. Here is where your membership in the airline's VIP club proves its value. Sign in at the club and give your ticket to the attendant, who will obtain your boarding pass while you relax and read the *Wall Street Journal*. On some airlines the attendant can also get your boarding pass for the return flight, making it possible for you to arrive at the airport at the last minute.

Last-minute arrivals are practical only if you have learned how to travel light. It is always evident who the inexperienced travelers are: They are the worried-looking souls milling about the baggage area waiting for their luggage to arrive. Experienced travelers never check their baggage, especially on overseas flights, where they don't want to be caught at the end of the line for the customs inspector. An experienced traveler has a light-weight suitcase and a briefcase; that is all. The suitcase goes under the seat or in the overhead rack and the briefcase provides papers to work on or reading material to pass the time. Upon arrival, the experienced traveler goes directly to the taxi or limousine stand; he never has anyone meet him because flight schedules are too erratic and airports too crowded to make that procedure feasible. While the others are still fighting for their luggage the experienced traveler is halfway to his destination, relaxing in the back seat of a taxi or limousine.

If you obtain a seat assignment in advance, you increase

the chances of obtaining a window seat. A window seat is not desired for the view since you probably won't be able to see anything through the clouds or the smog; it is preferred because people will not be crawling over you and passing food and coffee over your $350 English woolen suit. The airlines will pay for any mishaps to your clothing, but that is small consolation when you are scheduled to go directly from the airport to a meeting with the regional vice president and you are sporting a large coffee stain across your lap. The only safe seat is against the window, where the bulkhead can also be used as a headrest, if you are capable of sleeping on an airplane.

If you fly frequently, you should get a seating chart of the various aircraft flown by the airlines you use. The seating charts will help you in selecting your preassigned seat. You will not be able to get a first-row seat assigned in advance; those are reserved for children and others needing help. Try to obtain a seat in a row that has an emergency exit. There is slightly more leg room in those rows and usually the seats in front cannot be reclined fully so as to allow full access to the exit. The first rows and the exit rows are the only ones in which you can hope to avoid the sardine sensation of coach travel. However, if you do secure a seat in the first row, be prepared to share it with an infant or an elderly person whose plaintive requests of the flight attendant may impel you to provide assistance.

Airline VIP Clubs

These institutions are a must for the business traveler. The cost is modest and each club offers an oasis of quiet surroundings, carpeted lounges, comfortable easy chairs and sofas, free coffee, an uncrowded bar area, magazines and newspapers, telephones on desks to make note-taking easy, meeting rooms for conferences with clients or colleagues, and helpful attendants to make reservations or provide boarding passes. Conference rooms should be reserved in advance. Many travelers belong to several clubs because no one airline has clubs in all major cities. The best strategy is to select a club from an airline that flies primarily East—West, such as TWA, United, or American, and then supplement it with a club from a North–South airline, such as Delta or Eastern. More than 47 percent of the companies in the AMA survey paid for this amenity for their executives; however, few of those will pay for more than one club. If the company won't pick up the cost, bury it somewhere else in your expense account.

Here is a listing of some of the clubs with relevant information. American Airlines (Admiral's Club) has fifteen lounges in the United States which offer assistance in making reservations, selecting seats, and getting boarding passes. There is complimentary coffee and tea, free local phone calls, magazines, newspapers, conference rooms, and bar service. Members can bring in up to four guests at a time at no charge. There is a $40 initiation fee and an annual charge of $60.

Trans World Airlines (Ambassador Club) has twenty-seven lounges in the United States and overseas. They provide essentially the same services as above and also free juice and pastry in the morning. Special luggage tags are provided at no charge. The initiation fee is $25 and the annual membership charge is $45.

Pan American World Airways (Clipper Club) has twenty-nine lounges, most of them located overseas. They offer free drinks in addition to the standard services. The initiation fee is $25 and the yearly charge is $65.

Continental Airlines (Presidents Club) has seven lounges, all in the United States, offering the standard services. Emulating Pan Am, the drinks are on the house. There is a $40 initiation fee and the annual charge is $50.

United Airlines (Red Carpet Club) has nineteen lounges, all in the United States, which offer the standard services (no free drinks). There is a $50 initiation fee and a yearly charge of $60.

Northwest Orient (Top Flight Club) has seventeen lounges in the United States and the Far East. The standard services are supplemented by free beer and wine, and in some locations, free drinks. First class passengers who are not members have access to the club. There is no fee; membership is granted to steady customers of Northwest.

Travel with a Spouse

The lot of the executive traveler is not a happy one. The pace is such that in even the most enticing locale about all that is seen is the inside of the air terminal, the local Sheraton or Hilton, and occasionally a quick taxi ride through town to a restaurant of local fame. Almost invariably, meals on the road will be mediocre, saved only by the double martinis before, during, and after dinner. Experienced travelers have long since ceased paying attention to the repute of out-of-town restaurants. Almost without exception those inflated culinary reputations were achieved twenty years and three owners ago. The wisest course in dining out in a strange town is to ask about for the better Italian, Chinese, or Mexican restaurants and then check the names against the *Holiday* magazine or other listing of outstanding restaurants. If a restaurant you have uncovered appears on one of those lists, cross it off and take your chances with one of the others. Ethnic restaurants offer the best hope for a decent meal in an alien city but beware of Italian restaurants that feature pizza, Chinese restaurants that proclaim Cantonese cooking, and Mexican restaurants where anything costs more than five dollars. In ethnic dining the rule is, the more it costs, the worse it tastes. The meals in ethnic restaurants may not always be memorable, but at least you can be reasonably certain that the entrée was not shipped frozen to the chef to be zapped by the microwave just before the waiter delivers it to you with a flourish.

Business travel disappoints in other ways. Romantic encounters exist mainly in the fevered imagination of junior executives panting for their first out-of-town assignment. The reality of most evenings away from home is a hamburger and Heineken sent up from room service and an old movie on the telly. I've had more excitement at a Women's Christian Temperance meeting in Evanston, Illinois, than I found most nights on the road. Executive travelers are not imperiled by excessive partying but by terminal boredom.

The answer for many executives is to travel with their spouses as often as possible. Unfortunately, the necessity for two incomes or the presence of children makes this difficult for many executives, but with careful planning it can often be accomplished. Once the problem of time allocation has been solved, the problem of paying for the spouse must be met. Oddly enough this is one area in which there don't seem to be any cutbacks due to present business conditions. Almost 50 percent of the companies reporting to the AMA said they regularly paid for the travel expenses of a spouse accompanying an executive on a business trip, and 40 percent of that group placed no restrictions on the privilege. Of the companies imposing restrictions, most required that the spouse's presence be business-related or at the request of the company or occur no more than a specified number of times a year. Some of the companies imposing restrictions also paid for only part of the spouse's expenses. Allowing a spouse to accompany an executive to one convention a year appears to be the most popular form of this perk. Apparently, the reasoning is that if an executive is going to get into trouble, it is most likely to occur at a convention where serious business is usually not conducted and where ample time for misbehavior exists. The presence of a spouse at such time eases the concern of the board of directors and avoids nights of sleepless worry for them.

Travel with one's spouse is most often afforded to CEOs, but 11.4 percent of the companies also extend the privilege to middle managers. Banking and financial institutions obviously feel that their middle managers are immune to the blandishments of floozies or gigolos since only 3.6 percent of such firms will pay for a spouse's travel expenses. (In my

155

experience, however, the only group I have seen capable of matching a pack of dentists in uncontrolled revelry is a herd of bank managers.)

If your company is one that does not pay for spouse's travel, there are still ways of having your spouse join you at minimal cost. Your travel agent can usually find a discount air fare for you and your spouse and provide you with a dummy ticket for the regular full fare to use with your expense account. The difference in cost between two discount fares and one full fare is seldom very great. Your hotel charges will be virtually the same whether you are alone in the room or sharing it with your spouse. Meals present a problem, but the addition of your spouse's dinner to a restaurant check can be written off as a meal with a customer or supplier. Do not feel hesitant about adding such charges to your expense account; it is a small price for the company to pay to ensure your safety and ease of mind in an alien town.

Many executives combine overseas business trips with their annual vacation and include their spouses. Once again, by using discount fares and charging the company the full fare, the spouse can travel at little or no cost. Once the business part of the trip is concluded and the vacation begins, all costs are yours to bear. But in the interim considerable savings will have been achieved on air fares, meals, hotels, and rented cars.

Frequent-flyer Clubs

A new addition to the means by which spouses can accompany executives in their travels is the frequent-flyer clubs now available on most airlines. These promotional campaigns began in 1980 as a modest effort by Western Airlines to persuade business travelers to fly more often on Western. American Airlines followed suit in mid-1981 and the other airlines quickly offered their own plans. Under the various plans, as a traveler flies on a particular airline, credits accumulate which can be used for free flights, upgrading tickets, hotel and rental car discounts, and for various other goodies.

There is no cost to join any of the plans but there is usually some bookkeeping or other procedure necessary to make sure that you get credit for each flight. Most of the airlines only allow you to accumulate credits for one year but some have not yet set a time limit. An executive who travels often will find that credits accumulate rapidly; a friend of mine reached maximum credits with TWA in less than six months and is now well on his way to duplicating that with American. He will soon have two first-class tickets on both airlines to wherever they fly in the world. As a result and because he is a bachelor, he has found sudden popularity among his friends.

The only cloud in this pleasant picture is that a few companies have decided that the free airline tickets and other prizes should really belong to the companies that paid for the travel. Some executives have been directed to turn in their prize authorizations to their companies (Thank you, Mr. Scrooge), but most are refusing to do so on the reasonable argument that the prizes are small perks which compensate in a slight way for the onerousness of excessive travel.

Here is a brief description of the plans in operation as of the end of 1982:

American Airlines. You have twelve months to accumulate mileage. At 12,000 miles you can upgrade one ticket to first-class. At 25,000 miles you get 25 percent off on any round-trip ticket. After 50,000 miles you are entitled to a free first-class ticket anywhere American flies, plus a first-class upgrade for a companion. After 75,000 miles, you receive two first-class tickets.

British Airways. Mileage credits are shared with American and can be used on either airline. If the credits are used on British Airways, they are only applicable to flights between New York and London. After 20,000 miles you can fly the Concorde for the regular first-class fare. At 40,000 miles you are entitled to one free round-trip coach ticket. At 60,000 miles you are eligible for two coach tickets, or upgrading one coach seat to business class. You have twelve months in which to accumulate mileage.

Continental Airlines. Mileage also accumulates on New York Air and Texas International and free tickets can be used on any of the three airlines. Overnight stays at Hilton Hotels and rentals from National Car Rental also add to your mileage. At 40,000 miles you can get one free coach ticket, and at 70,000 miles two coach tickets. At 85,000 miles you receive two first-class tickets, which, like the awards at lower mileage levels, can only be used in the United States and Mexico. At 90,000 miles you receive two first-class tickets which can take you to Hawaii, Micronesia or Fiji. The program runs until March 31, 1984.

Delta. Mileage also accumulates on Air California and 35 regional commuter lines, and stays at Marriott Hotels or car rentals from Avis and Alamo can add to your mileage totals. You are also eligible to pay from $10 to $30 over the cost of a coach seat and receive a first-class seat on any flight.

Eastern. You have twelve months to accumulate your mileage and can add to the total with flights on five commuter lines in Florida. Credit for 1,000 miles is given on even short round-trips such as the shuttle between New York and Boston or Washington. At 10,000 miles you can upgrade to first-class. A 50 percent discount for one ticket is offered at 30,000 miles. At 40,000 miles you are entitled to a free coach ticket, and a first-class seat at 50,000 miles. Two coach tickets are offered at 70,000 miles and 90,000 miles brings two first-class seats.

Northwest Orient. The program is due to expire July 1, 1983 but will probably be extended. Instead of accumulating mileage, you get credit for the number of trips flown, regardless of distance. Ten one-way segments costing more than $100 each entitles you to a free coach ticket in the continental United States. Additional flights can qualify you for flights to Hawaii, the Far East or Europe.

Pan American. Mileage must be accumulated within twelve months but all travel is counted, including overseas flights. At the upper levels, 100,000 miles qualifies you for one free pass good for thirty days anywhere within the Pan Am system. If you live through it, 175,000 miles of travel entitles you to two first-class passes good for one month wherever Pan Am flies.

Republic. As with Northwest, credit is earned for flights, not mileage, and accumulates during one calendar year. Three round-trip flights earn a seat upgrade. Six trips earn a 50 percent discount; nine trips provides you with one free ticket on Republic's system. Fifteen trips earn two free tickets, but remember, Republic only flies within the continental United States.

Trans World Airways. Mileage is accumulated on domestic flights only, but free tickets can be used on overseas flights. The program has no expiration date and many fliers have been accumulating credits since 1981. At 50,000 miles you can receive a first-class ticket to any destination TWA flies in the U.S., Europe, or the Middle East, plus a second first-class ticket at the coach seat price. At 60,000 miles you are eligible for two free coach tickets. At 75,000 miles you earn two first-class tickets to a domestic destination, and at 95,000 miles you receive two first-class tickets to an overseas destination.

United. The big payoff comes at 75,000 miles when you receive two first-class tickets and a 50 percent weekend discount at Westin Hotels and Avis rental cars. United has not set an expiration date for the program.

Western Airlines. Mileage is accumulated during a calendar year and the upgrade to first class comes after only 5,000 miles. After 30,000 miles, you earn one free ticket to Mexico or Hawaii. At 150,000 miles there is something for the kiddies: a vacation for four anywhere Western flies, all on first-class tickets, and with an Avis car for five days.

Special Hotel Accommodations

Life on the road can be wearying and some hotels have recently begun to provide special accommodations for the business traveler that offer a level of comfort and convenience not found in the typical hotel room. Special accommodations are located on separate floors, usually at the top of each hotel, and provide rooms that, if not always larger than normal, are furnished more comfortably. For each bloc of special rooms there is a concierge on duty from early morning till late at night who can assist you in obtaining theatre tickets, making restaurant reservations, providing flight information, directing you to places of interest, arranging for secretarial services, and otherwise offering whatever assistance you need to make your stay more pleasant.

The Hilton, Sheraton, and Hyatt chains have done the most with the concept of special accommodations; many of their hotels in major cities offer the service, usually costing $20 to $40 more per night than a regular hotel room. Many business people consider the extra money well spent, and company auditors seldom question the expense. The Hyatt Hotels refer to their special accommodations as "Regency Clubs"; this originated in 1976 at the Regency Hyatt House in Atlanta. Currently, forty-four of the sixty-five deluxe Hyatt hotels in the United States have Regency Clubs, and if the two floors devoted to the club in the Hyatt on Union Square in San Francisco are typical, the harried traveler will find in them a welcome oasis. At the Hyatt on Union Square the club is on the thirty-second and thirty-third floors, with access to the floors possible only by the use of a special key on the elevator—a feature that provides a sense of security that is lacking in most hotels. As you exit the elevator, the concierge greets you, escorts you to your room, and inquires whether there is anything with which you need assistance. Fresh fruit will be in the room and down the hall is a small lounge with an honor bar where complimentary hors d'oeuvres are served each afternoon. Later in the evening complimentary cordials are served. In the morning a newspaper will be at your door and a complimentary continental breakfast available in the lounge. There is an express checkout service so you need not fret through the line at the cashier's counter. Perhaps best of all, you need not worry about having a room in the midst of a floor full of partying conventioneers whose boozy whoops and slamming doors at three A.M. are an essential part of their celebration.

An interesting variation on the theme of special accommodations is offered by Guest Quarters, a chain of eight hotels in the Southeast and Texas in which there are no individual rooms, only suites. Each suite has a living and dining area, a bedroom and a full kitchen. For executives traveling with families or for those who prefer to eat in, Guest Quarters offers a foodstuff delivery service. You leave your list of required foods with the bell captain and later that day it is all delivered to your room. There is a charge for the service based on the amount spent on food but it is well worth the convenience. You can then prepare your meals in your own kitchen and not have to chance the uncertain cuisine of a strange city. Don't forget to clean up using the dishwasher and put the dishes away! Guest Quarters are located in Washington, D.C. (two); Houston (two); Greensboro; Atlanta (two); and Alexandria, Virginia. If you stay over a Friday or Saturday night in Atlanta, the manager will be so pleased to have you that a basket of wine and cheese or champagne and fruit will magically appear in your room. The rates range from $57 per night for a single in Greensboro to $116 in D.C., which is only about $10 more than a single at one of the big hotel chains.

In the West, Midwest, and Southwest there are eighteen hotels that also offer only suites and are grandly named Granada Royale Hometels. There are no kitchens in the "Hometels" (surely one of the least felicitous neologisms in the innkeeper's lexicon), but each suite does have a living-room, bedroom, and a wet bar. The absence of a kitchen is hardly felt since a free buffet breakfast is available to each guest every morning. The developers have determined that it is cheaper to serve a buffet breakfast with its requirements for minimum help than to try to operate an in-house coffee shop with its attendant personnel and space problems. Even more revolutionary is the policy of serving un-limited free cocktails to each guest for two hours every afternoon. They calculate that the cost of free drinks only comes to 63¢ per suite per day; a more telling testament to the sobriety of American business people could hardly be imagined, but heaven help the Hometels if they are ever discovered by television folk or literary agents. Suites at the Hometels are priced from $45 to $70 per night, depending upon location, and are competitive with single rooms at better Holiday Inns.

Brock Residence Inns operates seven all-suite hotels in Colorado, Texas, Oklahoma, and Kansas and has plans to develop eleven more by 1984. Brock Inns come with com-plete kitchens and appeal greatly to transferred executives who need accommodations for an extended stay until their new residence is available. At a Brock Inn a studio with a kitchenette rents for about $80 a night; a two-bedroom suite will cost about $110.

Holiday Inns has decided there might be something to special accommodations; it announced in its annual report published in the spring of 1982 that the all-suite concept was one of the ways it intended to reach "the upper end of the mid-priced market." Stockholders were told that con-struction would soon start on Holiday Inns' first all-suite hotel, with future guests having a choice of one- or two-bedroom suites.

If your taste runs to something a bit more lavish and your expense account can handle it, a stay in one of the Pent-house Suites on the thirty-fourth floor of the Hyatt on Union Square in San Francisco will give you something to talk about with the folks back in Peoria. Instead of a con-cierge you will be greeted by your butler when you emerge from the elevator. Pierre or Brian or Dwain or Jacques will show you to your room and, while you sink into the sofa and tuck into a tray of hors d'oeuvres, will pour you a drink from among the decanters of gin, vodka, scotch, or bour-bon on the sideboard. In the refrigerator are bottles of Heineken, tonic water, and club soda or, if you prefer, the butler will uncork a bottle of vintage California white, chilled and served in a crystal glass from the stemware above the wet bar. After your clothes have been carefully put away, you may want to struggle to your feet and cross the thirty-six foot expanse of carpeting to the stereo system for some music as you gaze out on the skyline of San Francisco from the floor-to-ceiling windows. Beyond the stereo lies a bedroom the size of a badminton court with a concealed television set and terrycloth robes hanging in the closet. At one end of the dressing area is a shower roomy enough for six and at the other end, past the two washbasins, the vanity, and the makeup area is a sunken bath into which you and a companion can stretch out full length with room left for a mariachi band. (Note: Allow 45 minutes for the tub to fill.) If you are not careful, you can become addicted to the brownies that your butler leaves as a bedtime snack along with a glass of cold milk. In the morning you can order breakfast and have it served in the dining area as you watch while the fog rolls away to reveal the Golden Gate Bridge. The suite is more than ample size for business meetings of up to ten people, so there is no necessity to leave it unless you crave a stroll through Chinatown, which is less than a five-minute walk away. The price tag for these elegant digs is $600 a night but, what the hell, you only live once and it's time you stopped worrying about the company's cash flow.

If your concerns about cash flow cannot be controlled and you austerely turn your back upon special accommodations, I have one other suggestion. The typical hotel room has about as much charm as a small-town bus depot, with no place to sit and read in comfort or, heaven forbid, do some writing. A trick I picked up some years ago is to ask for the sitting room in a parlor suite. Instead of trying to live in a bedroom you are living in a living room, which, as the name implies, has got to be more comfortable. Rather than a room with nothing more than a bed, a small round table, and two vinyl chairs, you have a sofa, two easy chairs, a coffee table, a large table with chairs, and often a desk. The only disadvantage is that you sleep on a sofa bed, but that is usually no more uncomfortable than the plastic covered mattress found in too many hotels. Having a sitting room, you can conduct business in your room without having clients or customers eyeing the bed apprehensively. The cost is usually no more than a regular hotel room and the sense of being in an apartment rather than a high-rise barracks can make your stay much less irksome.

Extra Vacation Time

We finally come to a perk that doesn't cost the company anything and should be relatively easy to obtain. No one in the company need know anything about it except your boss. If you and he understand one another, there is no reason why you need be bound by company policy regarding vacations. Two weeks in a year is simply not sufficient to unwind from the pressure of modern business life. You need at least three weeks and preferably four to properly recharge your batteries. It is in your boss's interest as well as your own to have you provided with enough time away from your tasks to shed the everyday cares of your job and develop a new perspective. Come to an arrangement with your boss that allows you time to enjoy life and not just grind away at it. The usual procedure is to show your time away as "out of the office" or whatever similar phrase appears on the company time sheet. As long as the sheet is signed and approved by your boss, no one will question it.

To many, free time is the most valuable perk of all; it is one reason why airlines have no trouble getting applicants for jobs as airborne waitresses and why teaching still attracts so many even though the supply of teachers far exceeds the demand. Get all the vacation time you can, and use all of it. Without outside stimulation, the workaholic will eventually run out of ideas and turn his job into a series of repetitive tasks. Not only will his career stagnate, but the people reporting to him will cease to grow also.

Many companies are aware of this problem and insist

that employees take all their vacation time. They do this by refusing to allow employees to accrue vacation time from one year to the next and by not paying for unused vacation time. If an employee still doesn't take a vacation, the company may begin to wonder whether he isn't becoming neurotically compulsive about his work—or perhaps dipping into the till. Banks insist that managers and head tellers take all their vacation time. They know that it is the devoted senior employee who hasn't taken a vacation in ten years who is usually manipulating the books. By forcing vacations, a bank provides an opportunity for other persons to check the books without causing ill feelings.

An extra week or two of vacation each year will also improve your marriage and the relationship with your children. You may not be able to travel four full weeks every year, but even a week at home twice a year can be immensely beneficial when added to your normal vacation travels.

Don't worry about what will happen to your department while you're gone. As long as you don't stay away for a month at a time, no one will start to wonder about your absence. Two or three brief vacations during the year would be of much more benefit to you than a single extended absence, especially if you plan to take a four-week trip to Europe and see nine countries in 30 days (a not uncommon itinerary in these days of high-speed travel). The purpose of a vacation is to reduce the stress and tension of your life, not add to it. You may find it necessary to be a hard-driving executive, but there is no reason to carry that attitude into your vacation time. Relax, take things easy, and enjoy yourself. Space out your vacations so that the beneficial effects are spread over the course of a year and not concentrated into one frantic period each summer.

There is another reason to avoid long absences from your office. Everyone knows that no one is indispensable, but there's no reason to demonstrate how beautifully your department gets along without you. I was once acquainted with the head of an art and design department who for some years had been planning an extended European vacation with her husband. It was to be the trip of a lifetime, with visits to the art treasures of Italy and France combined with leisurely drives through Switzerland and the Austrian Tyrol. They had both accrued their vacation time so that the trip could last six full weeks. Susan returned to her job filled with ecstatic stories of museums and cathedrals and snow-capped alpine peaks that left her co-workers breathless with envy. What no one told Susan was that while she was away, decisions had had to be made on a number of important projects involving her department. Susan's assistant grasped the reins of leadership and impressed everyone with her analytical powers and the high quality of work that she was able to extract from the department in Susan's absence. The assistant heretofore had been considered young and inexperienced, but now she came to be regarded quite favorably—especially when the assistant's cooperative attitude was contrasted with Susan's somewhat abrasive insistence that quality and perfection of work were more important than meeting deadlines. Susan's boss looked at the situation and decided he preferred to sacrifice some of the perfection in the art and design work in exchange for increased intradepartmental harmony. The decision was made easier by the knowledge he would be saving almost $20,000 a year in the difference in salaries. Susan was asked to find other employment, and her assistant was appointed to replace her.

Even CEOs can encounter difficulty because of absences. Fletcher Byrom, former CEO of Koppers Company, is as *Forbes* magazine described him, "A man of protean interests. . . ." Byrom was often absent from Koppers, not entirely because of vacations but also because of his myriad outside interests. In addition to his duties at Koppers, Byrom was chairman of the Committee for Economic Development, a much-in-demand lecturer, a former chairman of The Conference Board, and the head of AT Technology, a nonprofit group promoting the spread of technology. When Koppers' return on equity dropped from 15.8 percent to 7.2

percent in the space of two years, the board of directors felt that a CEO was needed who could give the company his full attention. Byrom agreed and voluntarily retired two years early to teach and write. Absence doth not make a director's heart grow fonder.

Sabbatical Leaves

The competition for engineering talent is fierce in Silicon Valley. Engineers in hot fields such as integrated circuits or laser research frequently hop from one company to another. The wooing of engineers is constant and has all the subtlety of the use of liquid silicon by a Hollywood starlet. One of the side effects of this promiscuous job hopping has been the incentive for companies to work hard at keeping their employees. The high-tech companies south of San Francisco offer an array of benefits and perks unrivaled in American business. Stock options are often available down to the factory level, although they are designed not so much to reward as to retain valued employees; at most companies you have to hang in there for at least five years to cash in. Health clubs and hot tubs are standard, and it is an inspiring sight to observe those in charge of America's response to the Japanese challenge sporting after hours in the company hot tub while powerful jets lash the water to foam.

Tandem Corporation is one of the fastest growing of the high-tech companies and its success is based on a simple fact: Computers break down. Tandem meets this problem by selling every customer two computers; when one breaks down, the other takes over. The cost to the customer is doubled, but Tandem's simple solution has been welcomed by thousands of computer buyers. Just think how happy the automobile companies would be if every time you needed a car you bought two so that when the first one was in the repair shop you had a backup available. Tandem demonstrates its unorthodox thinking in other ways: Instead of a company hot tub they have a company swimming pool. It is questionable whether the pool actually provides more exercise than nearby company hot tubs, since the pool's main function seems to be to serve as a focal point around which the Friday afternoon beer busts can revolve, and to offer a suitably wet environment into which vice presidents can be pushed. Tandem apparently accepts the thesis of Professor Edward Feigenbaum as quoted in *Fortune* magazine regarding the retention of engineering talent: "Once you have one of these guys, you don't want to lose him. You have to coddle these people." Part of the coddling process at Tandem is a fully paid, six-week sabbatical every four years. This is in addition to any regular vacation time that has been earned. An employee on sabbatical may spend the time in any way he chooses; it need not be related to his work, and he does not have to account for his activity to anyone. Tandemites have disappeared into the mountains of Nepal on sabbatical and into a school of Cordon Bleu cooking. So far, all have returned safely from their sabbaticals and presumably begun marking off their calendars until the next. Tandem still loses some people it would prefer to keep, but its attrition rate is less than that for most companies in its industry and some of that success is due to its sabbatical-leave program.

For ten years Xerox has had an even more extensive sabbatical-leave program, although at Xerox it is much less free-wheeling than at Tandem. The program at Xerox is referred to as "social service leave" and can only be done in conjunction with a nonprofit, nonpolitical organization. Any Xerox employee with at least three years service is entitled to apply in writing for leave. The applications usually run fifty to two hundred per year, with fifteen to twenty or so approved each year. The applications are reviewed and selections are made by a committee of employees, seven to eleven in number, none of whom is a vice president or a corporate officer. The selection committee usually includes a member or two who has been on leave and who can help evaluate the practicality of the applications. Social service leave can range from three months to one year, and during that time the employee is paid full salary and all benefits are continued. Upon return, each employee is guaranteed an equal or better job than the one he left. Initially, a manager or two tried to delay or prevent the leave of an employee, but denials must be justified up to the CEO, and all such efforts were unsuccessful. No one has ever been denied leave, and managers no longer make an effort to alter the decisions of the selection committee. Those taking leave range from janitors in the factories to vice presidents. A few have returned to their old job and then decided that their service work was more rewarding and left Xerox to pursue it full time. Most have returned feeling their leave time was well spent and that the experience had a positive effect on their lives and their careers. Those on leave have joined community service organizations working with convicts, drug addicts, handicapped persons, the sick and injured, blind people, Indians, minorities, and poor people. Xerox seems well satisfied with the program, and it serves as an example of the kind of corporate and personal voluntarism that is usually more effective than impersonal government entitlement programs.

To no one's surprise the American Management Association found that "The fully paid sabbatical is not a benefit that is widely granted. . . ." Only seventeen companies, or 2.3 percent of those in the survey, allowed sabbatical leave by their employees. The length of time permitted by various companies is as follows:

Number of Companies	Sabbatical Leave Time Allowed
2	2 months
4	6 months
6	12 months
5	Individually determined

Seven of the companies grant the perk to all executives; the others restrict it to corporate officers.

Tickets to Events

The only activity receiving more corporate support than The United Way is professional sports. Every new stadium has a circle of enclosed suites from which games can be watched without suffering the discomfort of the elements or the noise of the crowd. Sound-proofed and so far from the field as to render the participants specks in the distance, each suite is furnished with multiple television sets so that the residents can follow events on the playing surface. Each is equipped with a wet bar and a well-stocked refrigerator, providing the principal reason for its occupancy. The annual rental for a suite ranges from $20,000 to $100,000 depending on the stadium, the size, and the location, but the cost is written off as a business expense.

Usually, only CEOs and top corporate officers are to be found in corporate suites, but companies are still in the habit of also buying up blocs of season tickets for regular seats. Those tickets are often available to corporate employees below the level of vice president. Your company probably has such seats for whatever professional sports activity your city offers. Availability is on the basis of rank, with the CEO having first call on the seats and then down through the intervening levels of management until you are reached. Often the seats go unused since executives travel a great deal and cannot give sporting events the attention they deserve.

In most companies one person is designated the distributor for unclaimed seats and customarily takes care of his friends, both inside and outside the company, rather than seeking deserving employees upon whom to bestow his largesse. Not infrequently, the distributor considers unclaimed seats as a personal perk and sells them to scalpers. It's time for you to take advantage of this corporate perk, especially if you don't have an expense account to which you can charge similar expenses. You have two choices, either make a friend of the distributor or enlist your boss's support. The second alternative is more feasible, since the distributor undoubtedly has more friends than he presently can handle. The distributor is probably outranked by your boss who, if he requests tickets, can hardly be refused. Your boss can pass the tickets on, and you sample one of the advantages of working for a big corporation.

Many companies also have available tickets to the theater or other events of interest. A play, concert, symphony, or ballet can offer an evening's divertissement that is often quite enjoyable. Even outside New York the quality of performing arts in this country is astonishingly high and a ticket to a local event can be a richly rewarding evening. Tickets to nonsporting events are usually more readily available and often the good offices of your boss are not necessary to secure them. All it takes is a little diligence on your part to seek out the dispenser of such tickets and to inquire on a regular basis as to what is available. Half the time this perk is unused in a company because most of the people don't know about it and, of those who do, most couldn't care less.

In addition to events in the world of performing arts, companies occasionally have tickets for events of a more specialized nature. A personal experience may help you in judging the value of such offerings. While still in the corporate world I was approached one day by the vice president of personnel offering two tickets to a formal dinner dance to be given that Saturday night in the Grand Ballroom of the Sheraton Centre. The affair was sponsored by a prominent charitable appeal that was honoring one of our company's executives as Man of the Year. Since one of its own was being honored, the company felt obliged to purchase eight full tables of tickets at $250 per seat. The personnel department was then faced with the task of finding users for the tickets.

I said I would be happy to attend but the last tuxedo I had worn had been returned immediately after the prom. I was told that the company honor was at stake and I should rent a tuxedo and whatever else was required and charge it to the company. With sly cunning I asked about taxis and a corsage. "Yes, yes," was the impatient reply, "anything you need, just make sure you show up." It did not occur to me to inquire why it appeared so difficult to give away tickets to an event that gave promise of being the highlight of the year, at least on my social calendar, replete as it was with television game shows.

I scooted over to a rental shop on 54th street and allowed as how I was in the market for a tuxedo. "We have them in all price ranges," was the reply.

"Let me have the best," I countered grandly. "My company is picking up the tab."

With a knowing smile the salesman vanished behind a curtain to appear a moment later with a tuxedo of such splendor as would cause Fred Astaire to weep with envy. I shrugged into the jacket and it hung from my frame as if molded by the finest tailor on Savile Row. The jacket was followed by matching pants and vest and a shirt of luminous whiteness. The rental cost was staggering but I swallowed my qualms, reasoning that the company would not want to be embarrassed by my appearing in a tuxedo less than fitting for such an occasion. While being measured for cuff length I called my wife and told her the good news. She stammered in gratitude for my thinking of her first, and I considered again how satisfying it was to belong to one of the Fortune 500.

The cab driver actually mumbled something I took for a thank you when we alighted in front of the hotel, and as we mounted the wide steps my wife was the cynosure of every eye. We entered the reception area of the ballroom, where a sea of bodies swirled about the tables, attacking the food with a spirit not seen since the Donner party reached Sacramento.

As my wife and I approached the bar, the press of bodies parted before us as had the Red Sea before the Israelites. I suddenly realized that the hall was filled with junior typists, file clerks, management trainees, college-age scions of corporate executives, receptionists, and assorted other nonexecutive types. Their staring eyes briefly unnerved me and I turned to my wife in amazement and whispered, "They all think we're Somebody."

"I *am* Somebody," she replied with certainty and, looking at her, I had to agree.

We entered the ballroom and looking about, I realized that other companies had experienced even more difficulty than mine in disposing of their tickets.

A master of ceremonies stepped to the microphone, welcomed us and announced there were some people on the dais whose efforts on behalf of the charity deserved recognition. The M.C. introduced a portly gentleman at the far end of the dais and described his work in the vineyards of philanthropy, his struggle to overcome an underprivileged childhood, his wife and her beneficent activities, his children and their accomplishments in the professional world, and the inspiration of his parents, who taught him love for humankind, the arts, and small animals. This took the better part of seven minutes. Twenty minutes later I sat in stunned disbelief as I saw that every person on the dais— which ran the full length of the room—was to be introduced in the same fulsome manner. The introductions were finally ended and dinner was served at eleven o'clock, an hour that is adjudged suitable for the evening repast in Madrid but in my neighborhood is long past the time for repose.

The high point of the evening came after a fifteen-minute introduction of the Man of the Year, whom I had often seen about the corridors of the company and who was unrecognizable from the description given by the master of ceremonies. After a standing ovation, in which I was unable to participate, the Man of the Year thanked those who had selected him for his signal honor and recited an interminable litany of praise for all those who had helped him in his life. He modestly accepted the acclaim of the throng, and with no pause for reflection a band began to play. The youthful members of the audience flung themselves onto the dance floor as the pounding beat of disco music filled the hall. I and a few others rendered comatose by the wine and the speeches sat nailed to our seats while around us the flailing limbs of avid discoists threatened permanent injury.

After an unknown period of time my wife returned from the dance floor flushed with happiness and introduced me to her dancing partner, who shook my hand with the grave courtesy accorded the terminally ill. Shortly thereafter, my eyes fighting sleep, I found myself in a taxi bearing us homeward, my only thought to retain consciousness until the bedroom was reached. I paid the cabby in a manner learned in foreign lands, a handful of currency extended for his selection. I resolved never again to appear in public wearing a tuxedo, unless of course I am to be on the dais where it will be my turn to be the borer rather than the bored.

— 10 —

Image and Status

I've known Harry for fifteen years and have always enjoyed being around him. He's cheerful and enthusiastic and works as hard as anybody I know. He was one of the most effective salesmen his company ever had and when he was made a division manager performed equally well in that position. He was brought into the home office as a product manager and later appointed sales manager for a subsidiary company. Everyone agrees that Harry has done outstanding work in whatever job he had. But no one quite knows what to do with Harry because he looks and acts so disorganized. His office is a shambles. He is tall and good-looking but his shirttails usually protrude from the back of his trousers and his suits, while of good quality, look as if they were rolled into a ball after each wearing. Harry is in constant motion, charging from one task to another and from one meeting to another, habitually late and always appearing frazzled. Harry cares nothing for appearances and at a business lunch will often order chocolate milk. When I asked him about this he responded, "I like it. Why shouldn't I order it?"

The answer to Harry's question and the reaction to much of his behavior is the same: "Because it isn't good for your image." Harry is approaching forty and he now dresses with a bit more care and organizes his activities a little better, but he still does not present the image of a corporate vice president. This might not be fatal if he were working for a high-tech company in the laid-back land of Silicon Valley, but Harry works for a $4-billion conglomerate in New York City. His ability, energy and dedication should have made him a vice president years ago, but his image may make that goal impossible.

In large corporations promotions below the vice president level are usually handled within a department, and the criteria revolve around job performance and perceived ability to manage others. In considering candidates for a vice president's slot, another criterion is added. The president looks at each candidate and says to himself, "When this person makes a presentation to the board or attends a meeting of the executive staff, is his manner or appearance going to make me look bad?" Competence is still a critical factor, but competence alone is seldom enough. Ability and image must be joined in order to create a fully realized corporate career.

If you are a vice president and austerely eschew the perks of your office, others, both above and below you, will begin treating you as if you are not a vice president. If that begins to happen, it becomes a self-fulfilling prophecy; as Eliza Doolittle learned, if you are treated like a duchess you become a duchess, while if you are treated like a flower girl you stay a flower girl. Skilled perks players know that failing to demand all the perks of their position soon endangers that position.

Your Office

The first and perhaps most important element in establishing your status and polishing your image is your office. In the military, rank is immediately known by the insignia on each person's uniform; in the corporate world, rank is denoted by a person's office. There are perks players who within 30 seconds of entering someone's office will know that person's exact rank in his company and within 5 percent of his salary. The size, location, and furnishings of an office tell as much about its occupant as his personnel file.

Corporate facilities managers know that any time there is a reorganization or relocation of a department, the struggle for prestige office space will be bitter and hard-fought. Each manager will present the most forceful arguments as to why his work requires a corner office or at least one that is somewhat larger than those of his peers. The vehemence with which the arguments are presented is a reflection of the importance of one's office as a symbol of one's status rather than a need for a particular office in order to do the job better.

Once the disputes over space have been settled, the struggle over furnishings begins. Did you get a credenza behind your desk? If your peers each have one, you had better make sure you get one also. Don't accept the story that the company is temporarily one credenza short; let someone else do without. Raise a fuss until a credenza is found for you; otherwise it will be months and months before they get around to supplying you with one, and by that time there may be an austerity drive on and all furniture purchases frozen. The same principle applies to sofas, chairs, coffee tables, or anything else that might go into your office. This is not the time to be Mr. Good Guy. If you want to receive all the things to which you are entitled, you are going to have to fight for them. If you don't, your peers are going to gain a leg up in the Status Game, which gives them an advantage on you in a more important activity, the Promotion Game.

The Buffalo Organization for Social and Technological Innovation (BOSTI) is a nonprofit group studying office productivity. They surveyed 4,000 white-collar workers to identify the indicators of status that an office conveys. The results were, in order of descending importance:

1. Size of the office
2. Location
   a. Corner
   b. Many windows
   c. Proximity to higher-ups

3. Amount of furniture
4. A door for privacy
5. Quality of furniture
6. Devices
   a. Telephones
   b. Computer terminals
7. Personal articles
   a. Art works
   b. Plants

Measure your own office against those of your peers using the criteria above. If you find your office consistently rates low, you are losing important points in the Status Game. More seriously, you are unnecessarily hampering your efforts to move up the corporate ladder. You have acquiesced in a series of actions that tell the world you are not as important as your peers; that is not a message you should be transmitting, unless you like your little niche in the world and wouldn't leave it for anything.

In examining BOSTI's criteria, I have to believe the 4,000 white-collar workers were concentrated at the lower levels of management and are unaware of an office feature of much concern to corporate officers. Although the rankings are essentially accurate, they omit one office accoutrement that may outrank a corner location in terms of desirability: the private bathroom. At one company I know, a division president yearned for a private bathroom, a status symbol possessed by only six other persons in the corporation, all of whom were housed in the headquarters building. Since the division president's office was located in the offices of a subsidiary, there was an opportunity to acquire a private washroom as part of a general remodeling. Unfortunately, the building was an older one with limited access to plumbing lines, and to extend them to the corner where the division president's office was located would have added enormously to the remodeling cost. Hundreds of man-hours were spent trying to solve the problem of how to run the plumbing lines without virtually tearing the building apart, but there was no way to do it. The division president was faced with the choice of moving his office away from his prestigious corner location to a spot closer to the plumbing or doing without the private bathroom. He chose to do without and can still be found democratically mingling with the others in the communal washroom. But for those who have a private bathroom, what a sense of distinction is felt as they step from their shower, clean and refreshed, while their underlings are becoming more sweaty and grimy as the day proceeds.

The IBM Research Center in Yorktown Heights, New York, has avoided most of the problems associated with offices. The building is a curving structure of stone and glass and sets on a knoll surrounded by lawn and forest. Each office is exactly the same size and furnished in exactly the same way. The maneuvering for offices with windows had been avoided by placing the corridors along the outside walls: No one gets a window. One end of the building is occupied by a cafeteria with a ceiling that goes up to the roof, and the other end is taken up by storage and service areas; the result is no corner offices. With the jockeying for office status eliminated, IBM is now in position to meet the challenges of the Computer Age.

Earlier, we spoke of allies you need to win the Perks Game and mentioned travel agents and, within your company, your boss and the person auditing your expenses. There are other allies within your company who can be helpful; one is the facilities manager or whoever is in charge of assigning space, allocating furniture, arranging for telephones, and the other services that keep a company functioning smoothly. Make an effort to know this person; take him to lunch once in a while and provide a sympathetic ear. Whoever has that job deals with nothing but headaches all day long. A little sympathetic listening on your part can pay off handsomely at some point in the future.

Do not try to go around the facilities manager or ignore him. I learned that lesson shortly after I received my first assignment as a manager in my company's home office. I was assigned a pleasant office with not one but two windows, carpeting on the floor, and even pictures on the walls. I leaned back in my chair and surveyed my domain and was content. Until I went into the office of the manager next door and saw that he had a sofa and a low coffee table. My contentment faded and I resolved to obtain similar furnishings for myself. A quick survey of the floor showed a sofa sitting in solitary splendor opposite the elevators. It seemed to be serving no purpose and certainly didn't belong to anyone. I enlisted the aid of one of my subordinates and we carried the sofa into my office where it made a handsome addition to the decor. Early the next morning, two burly handymen entered my office and wordlessly picked up the sofa to return it to its previous home. While I was pondering my next move I received a visit from my boss who told me of a phone call he had received from the facilities manager. My boss politely informed me that any additions to my office furnishings had to be approved by the facilities manager. Thanking him for his guidance I called the facilities manager and was icily informed that any hope I had of acquiring additional office furnishings had vanished with my precipitate action. Until the day I left that company my office was as Spartan as a monk's cell, but I had learned a useful lesson.

Should you think the emphasis on the importance of your office as a symbol of your status is overdone, I offer the following examples that illustrate the attitude of successful people toward their offices. Some years ago in Boston I had reason to visit the offices of F. Lee Bailey, the noted criminal lawyer. Since Mr. Bailey was out at the time I was permitted a peek into his private office. I entered a long, dimly lit room with dark, paneled walls and carefully draped windows. The deep carpet stretched from the entrance to the distant horizon where one could make out a large mahogany desk and high-backed leather chair. The only direct illumination in that vast chamber was from a ceiling fixture directly over the desk, bathing it in a halo of light. The desk and chair were elevated one step up from the rest of the room to afford a commanding view of the terrain. Instinctively, I bowed as I reverently backed from the room, not daring to breathe until I was safely outside. I pitied the witness or opposing counsel forced to enter that room, traverse the carpet, and step up to await their fate from the man behind the desk. It was apparent that Mr. Bailey gave as much attention to the design of his office as he did to the preparation of his cases, and to the same end: to accomplish a desired result.

Douglas Nicholson is chairman of a subsidiary of Cushman and Wakefield, which deals with corporate clients on their building and office needs. According to *Fortune* magazine, Nicholson feels that a CEO is mostly involved in role playing: "He doesn't need equipment, he needs a stage set." If Mr. Nicholson is correct, Southern California should be the heartland of lavish executive offices since Hollywood determines so much of the culture there. Not surprisingly, Hollywood carries its design capabilities into the offices of studio heads. Ted Ashley retired recently as head of Warner Brothers and worked out of your basic movie mogul office. To approach Mr. Ashley, you entered a large, lavishly furnished foyer through a pair of massive, silver Art Deco doors with copper borders. Beyond the foyer was an inner sanctum with a fireplace, gray-flannel walls, and a desk with a glass base and a stainless steel top. Genuflection, while not required, certainly would not have been out of place.

Armand Hammer, CEO of Occidental Petroleum, felt the need for an office befitting his position as head of one of the world's major oil companies and retained an interior decorator to provide the finest executive suite in America. The top floor of the Occidental Oil building in Los Angeles (where else?) was completely done over to provide 16,000 square feet of luxurious appointments for Mr. Hammer and his six top assistants. In an ordinary office, 16,000 square feet of space would accommodate eighty persons, so one can assume that crowding will not be a problem for Dr.

Hammer and his associates. There are four private dining rooms (two with fireplaces—nights can get nippy in southern California), a kitchen, a board room, a formal reception area, and an art gallery. Dr. Hammer has a feeling for wood, so the floors are oak parquet and the walls paneled in walnut, except in the art gallery, where the wall covering is linen. The cost of the remodeling was a modest $1.5 million, a pittance considering the effect that has been achieved. Visitors must climb a circular stairway from the floor below to enter Dr. Hammer's private offices, and one must assume that, as a visitor mounts the staircase, in the background is heard the stirring sounds of Wagner's "Ascent of the Gods into Valhalla."

In New York City CEO offices tend to be less ostentatious but probably no less costly. William Paley although retired still shares the top floor of the CBS Building with Thomas Wyman, company president, and a covey of efficient secretaries. A private elevator whisks the dazzled visitor to the thirty-fifth floor, where he enters a world of taste and refinement. The spacious reception area is carpeted from wall to wall in expensive broadloom. Deep, richly covered sofas are placed so as to provide several discreet waiting areas. The subdued lighting and dark, paneled walls create an atmosphere in which one speaks in lowered tones. The receptionist buzzes Mr. Paley's office (no telephones ring on the thirty-fifth floor; just an occasional quiet buzzing is heard) and Mr. Paley's secretary's secretary emerges to lead you inward. She presents you to Mr. Paley's secretary, who opens the door to the inner office and introduces you with quiet graciousness. Windows on two sides provide light to the chamber, which is large enough for a brisk game of squash. You know instinctively that the paintings on the walls are originals and that the area rugs are genuine Orientals. Even to the untutored eye the furniture is obviously made up either of valuable antiques or of the finest from traditional furniture makers. A display of antique microphones from the early days of radio sits atop a polished mahogany chest. As you gaze about, a voice in your ear whispers, "Money, power, success! This is what the game is all about."

Your Private Secretary

On a regular basis over the past five years articles have appeared in business magazines asking, "What's Delaying the Office of the Future?" The theme of each article is the same: Equipment is available to increase office productivity but companies are slow to take advantage of it. Manufacturers of word processors and computer-based communication systems shake their heads in bewilderment; for every sale there are a hundred other companies who just can't seem to make a decision. Explanations for the reluctance of businesses to accept office automation range from the initial cost (admittedly high but quickly recovered in productivity savings) to statements that managers will never accept a system that requires them to operate terminals (yet everyone knows that managers always resist change but then get accustomed to it).

The reason managers are resisting automation in their offices has little to do with cost or resistance to change and a lot to do with their image of themselves as important persons. A manager in an automated office is almost certainly going to share a secretary with one or more other managers because the only way the cost of these systems can be justified is by showing a reduction in secretarial and clerical staffs. After Lee Pharmaceuticals installed personal computers the secretarial staff was reduced by 50 percent. Why should a manager embrace a new development that is going to cost him one of his most cherished status symbols and replace it with something that is going to force him to learn new ways of doing things?

Automation equipment manufacturers should be striving to make their terminals a mark of *status* so that the loss of one status symbol, the private secretary, can be replaced by another, the personal computer terminal. The basic concept in selling is showing how your product or service can help the customer solve a problem. What problem does a manager have that a word processor or computer-based communication system is going to solve? The word processor allows typing to be done faster and with fewer errors, but speed and accuracy aren't the manager's problems; they're the concern of his secretary. If she has too much typing to do, she can always get an assistant, enhancing both her status and that of her manager, or they can hire someone on a temporary basis to help with the typing. If the manager has trouble reaching someone on the telephone, he can always have his secretary keep trying or, in an emergency, send the secretary to the other person's office. In neither situation is there a problem that the manager feels so acutely as to make him want to automate his office at the risk of losing one of his most important symbols of success, his private secretary.

The nasty little secret of business life is that it is difficult for most managers to provide work sufficient to keep an efficient secretary busy seven to eight hours a day. Private secretaries can be justified only for the most compulsive workaholics who bring a briefcase full of work to the office each morning. A rule of thumb is that every hour your secretary works on business matters requires an hour of your time to prepare the work and check it afterwards. Therefore, if your secretary is to be fully occupied each day, you will have time for nothing except preparing her assignments. This is why secretaries spend so much of their time rearranging files, running errands for their bosses, and attending to their bosses' private affairs. The secretaries who are fully occupied each day are either woefully inefficient or else they have taken over many of their bosses' responsibilities and are, in effect, assistant department heads. Secretaries between those two extremes spend much of their time looking for something to do. In many offices, especially in New York, the search for work has been abandoned and secretaries spend considerable time each day reading novels and doing crossword puzzles. Private secretaries are a perk provided by a company so that an executive can look into the mirror each morning and say, "I'm an important person. I've got a private secretary to prove it."

As inflation and the recession reduce company earnings, many executives find themselves sharing a secretary. For those recently promoted, who never had a secretary, this presents no problem. For those accustomed to a private secretary, the communal secretary or, even worse, nothing but a receptionist and access to the typing pool can be a bitter pill to swallow. No longer can Mr. Executive say, "I'll send my secretary right over to pick it up," and know that his secretary will be available to impress the other person with the forces at his command. Oh, the ignominy of being forced to personally lead a visitor from the reception area past the shabby filing cabinets and the odorous lavatories back to one's office! Every step of that trek tells the visitor more plainly than words that Mr. Executive is not a person of real consequence.

In today's business world a private secretary, as much as a corner office or any other perk, establishes your position as person of importance. Like the star on the collar of a general, a private secretary outside your office is a silent declaration of your rank.

If you do not yet have a secretary of your own, you should be working diligently to acquire one. Your best course is to take on more and more responsibility and generate longer and more frequent written reports. Overwork the secretary you share with assignments great in number and immense in scope; impose timetables impossible to be met and then sympathize with her—do not criticize her—when the work cannot be completed in time. Soon she will be down in the personnel office asking for a transfer or talking about leaving the company because of the burden of work. The other managers who share her with you will be complaining to your boss that they can never get any work done because you monopolize the secretary's time. Let the situation build for awhile and then suggest to your boss that you want to help correct the situation; the only remedy appears to be a secretary of your own.

If you already have a private secretary and the company is talking about automating the office, do not oppose the plan; in all likelihood persons above you have initiated the idea and will not listen sympathetically to opposition. Be one of the few managers to embrace the idea enthusiastically, thereby winning points for flexibility and a mature outlook from your superiors. In private lay plans to retain your secretary, because as sure as God made little green apples the company will pay for the new equipment by cutting back on the secretarial and clerical staffs.

Make your secretary indispensable to the operation of your department by having her serve as your de facto assistant. Make the typing and clerical functions of her job less important and delegate to her tasks that require research, analysis, recommendations, and lower-level decision making. When the winds of change blow through your office and the dust has settled, the office will be automated, the other managers will be sharing secretaries, but you will still have your own private secretary to maintain your now enhanced image. In addition, you will find to your surprise that your secretary is capable of much more than you thought and, lo and behold, you will be functioning more effectively as a manager. Automation is a wonderful thing but only when used properly; that means that automation should add to your status and the symbols of your rank, not detract from them.

The Chauffeured Limousine

Harold Geneen is a British-born accountant who favors rimless spectacles and a serious mien. He is not physically imposing, and in a crowd you might take him for a senior bank teller or a middle-level company auditor. In real life, Harold Geneen took a rag-tag collection of overseas telephone companies and built them into the most consistently successful of all conglomerates, ITT, with a twenty-year record of unbroken increases in earnings and profits. Geneen was famous for his monthly presidents' meetings where the heads of all ITT subsidiaries gathered in New York to review the results for each subsidiary in the previous month. Each subsidiary president had to explain any variations from budget, and woe to the man who did not have a convincing explanation. Geneen was not concerned about problems that might have arisen since problems are a natural part of business life. What was of concern was a problem that was unanticipated and for which a contingency plan did not exist. "Do not tell me that you fell behind because a dock strike in Barcelona prevented the unloading of the cement you needed. Why did you not anticipate such an event and have a contingency plan available?"

Geneen was merciless in his unmasking of faulty thinking or inadequate planning. He would dig and probe and burrow away until the hapless executive on trial had no defenses left. Geneen was not one to coddle the egos of his managers, and his questions and comments could be scathing as he exposed the weaknesses of a subordinate. The turnover among ITT division presidents was a concern to everyone except Geneen, as more than one $250,000-a-year-man broke under Geneen's version of The Inquisition and reportedly wept openly in the board room.

The wonder was that any of Geneen's lieutenants were able to bear up under the pressure; of those who stayed it was said, "Harold's got 'em by their limousines." For no matter what sort of humiliation had to be endured in the board room, after it was over each man stepped into his private limousine and leaned back in luxury as the chauffeur steered the vehicle away from the curb and into the press of traffic filled with other vehicles whose unimportant owners were by necessity their own drivers.

By the time each manager's destination was reached, he was once again the calm, confident successful person the world knew. When he alighted from his limousine to the envious stares of passersby and underlings, no trace of his ordeal could be detected. The soothing sensation of the limousine and the presence of the chauffeur had restored his self-image and he was prepared to face the world with the steely eye of one who has made it.

You will recall the tale of the division president who was appointed acting group president and came to enjoy the satisfactions of a chauffeur and limousine. There is a footnote to that story. When the division president was allowed to retain the limousine after returning to his previous position, the other division president in the group was extremely disturbed. With great force and considerable justification he advanced the proposition that if one division president in the group was entitled to a limousine, so was he. The limousineless executive was deaf to all pleas that he understand that this was an unusual circumstance and that the company could not very well take back a limousine from one who had grown accustomed to it. The response was that in that case he should be provided with a limousine also to even out the distribution of perks among equals. It was pointed out that it would be impossible to get the corporate president to approve another limousine for a division president because that would trigger off a stampede among the division presidents in the other groups. Deaf to all reason, the executive kept insisting that he be provided with a limousine. Finally, in order to restore harmony, the new group president approved a solution that satisfied all parties. The group had previously obtained approval for a new delivery van, with driver, to carry mail and packages between the various offices and plants of the group. Instead of a van, a limousine was purchased and put at the disposal of the other division president. The driver was provided with a uniform and dutifully picked up the executive each morning at his home, drove him to his office, and then returned him each evening. The executive had to agree that occasionally the driver and limousine had to be available during the day to make emergency deliveries among the group facilities. It was the sort of imaginative solution that has made American industry the envy of the world, and allowed the participants to get back to their essential tasks of managing a billion-dollar enterprise.

If you think the division president without a limousine made a fuss over something not terribly important, you would be mistaken. The limousine itself was perhaps not significant, but what it represented was worth all the commotion and the ill feelings that were generated. The executive without a limousine had to look ahead to a time when promotion to group president might again become available. At that time, if one candidate had a limousine and the other did not, it is almost certain that the executive with the limousine would be awarded the position because it would eliminate an unusual and troublesome situation: a division president with a limousine. By making him the group president, his possession of the limousine would be justified and there would no longer be a division president with a limousine. Order and balance would have been restored to the company list of perks.

The American Management Association found that chauffeurs are not commonly provided to executives except in billion-dollar corporations. The expectation is that the chauffeur and limousines are to be used only for business purposes, but most companies understand that personal use becomes an inevitable aspect of the perk. Few companies will object if the executive uses the limousine to take him to a dental appointment, but if the chauffeur is asked to return to the executive's home and drive his wife to a luncheon in town, eyebrows will be raised. The AMA found that 13.5 percent of the companies responding to the survey provided a chauffeur for their CEO. There were even 1 percent of the companies who provided chauffeurs for selected middle managers. I would anticipate that turnover among that 1 percent would be exceedingly low.

Another 7.1 percent of companies provided a part-time driver for their CEOs, and 1.5 percent for middle managers. Part-time drivers do not always imply a limousine; often the lower status of the driver is reflected in the vehicle, which is usually a Chrysler or an Oldsmobile. Also the part-time driver probably does not wear a uniform and undoubtedly is not properly instructed in the proper procedure for bowing an executive into and out of the car.

A recommended ploy for status enhancement is to suggest the use of the boss's driver and car when asked to make a hurried trip at the boss's request. The suggestion should be made in furtherance of the need for speed and certainty of arrival. If the ploy is successful and not overdone, you will be able to add to your status points on a regular basis.

Many suburban companies have drivers on call to ferry executives to and from the airports. Use this service rather than your own automobile even if it is a bit less convenient. You do not want your peers and superiors to lose sight of the fact that you are entitled by rank to the use of the company driver. Important executives do not chauffeur themselves for any reason, and you want to establish your place in that hierarchy.

The Company Jet

Some years ago I was a middle-level manager with Xerox Corporation when the company still had its corporate headquarters in Rochester. I was part of the Education Group, which had its offices on Madison Avenue and 58th Street in Manhattan. Early one morning, six or seven other managers and I were called into the personnel office and told we would be having lunch that day with C. Peter McColough, president of Xerox. There was a flutter from the group that sounded as if a flock of chickens had been suddenly roused from its sleep. My mind was in such a whirl that I barely heard the explanation that Mr. McColough wanted to visit with some of the people in the Education Group to get a feel for its problems and potential. We were told to report back to the personnel office at eleven-fifteen A.M.

I returned to my office to catch my breath and see whether my socks matched. I considered a flying visit to

Bancroft to purchase a new shirt and tie but discarded the idea; my suit, a closeout special from Robert Hall, was certain to give the game away no matter what else was worn. I settled for a quick dusting of my shoes with a paper towel from the men's room and a visit to the company library to see what I could learn about Mr. McColough. My recollection is that he is a Canadian who earned an M.B.A. at Harvard and prior to joining Xerox was with Consolidation Coal Company. At that time he was one of the youngest presidents of a major American corporation and known for his penetrating mind. I looked forward to our luncheon with some apprehension.

At eleven-fifteen we reassembled in the personnel office and were told that Mr. McColough's private jet had taken off some minutes earlier from Rochester bound for La-Guardia airport. The members of our group looked at each other in silent awe—a private jet? One of America's foremost business leaders was flying to New York in his private jet to have lunch with us! What could we say to Mr. Mc-Colough that could possibly make the trip worthwhile? We sat in silent anxiety as periodic reports arrived regarding Mr. McColough's progress. The jet was over Albany. The jet was approaching White Plains. The jet was in its final approach. The jet had touched down. The limousine was leaving the airport. The limousine was on the parkway. The limousine was on the Triborough Bridge. With that last announcement, a functionary of the personnel department brought us to our feet and checked off our names as he led us into the elevator. In double file we were marched west on 58th Street, across Fifth Avenue, and into the Oak Room of the Plaza Hotel, where a long table next to the wall awaited us.

The personnel assistant left and a waiter approached and asked for our drink orders. Dead silence. My God, what was the protocol? While waiting for the company president to arrive from his jet, do you order or do you wait for him? If you don't order, what do you do while you wait? If you do order, what drink is appropriate? I ordered iced tea.

191

The others gasped with relief and all ordered the same. Iced tea, the perfect solution: not a drink drink, but nevertheless something to set in front of us so that it appeared that we belonged in the Oak Room. We sat sipping our iced tea and contemplating the nature of a universe in which one man can command his own jet aircraft to take him wherever his fancy might lead. Suddenly, Mr. McColough was among us with an assistant to do the introductions.

The conversation for the next hour and a half was somewhat strained, but Mr. McColough proved to be a careful listener with a manner designed to put us at our ease. I remember none of the conversation except that someone asked Mr. McColough about the jet and he went into considerable detail as to its operation and how it was furnished as an office so that he could work while in the air, how it saved time for him and his top aides, how it was in almost constant use carrying executives all over the United States, how there was a full maintenance crew on the ground and two full-time pilots were always available, and how it could cruise at almost 600 miles per hour. Wow!

The meal ended with my eyes seeing little, fixed as they were on a distant cloud bank that my powerful jet would need to surmount as it carried me at almost the speed of sound to the next stop on my survey of the industrial empire which I ruled.

A large jet can cost up to $14 million, not including the cost of a custom-designed interior. Even a small jet will cost more than $2 million, but price is apparently not a deterrent to many companies. Fifty-five percent of the *Fortune* 1000 companies own one or more airplanes, with a total value of $3.21 billion. Marathon Oil may have the most, a fleet of twelve airplanes, but Kimberly-Clark is close behind with nine. United Technologies has five airplanes, including a Boeing 727 and a Boeing 737. Since the cost of operating a small jet totals about $40,000 per month, one can only imagine the annual costs for these companies.

The company jet is another device that lifts an executive out of the ordinary and into the rarefied strata of those who live and work as others do not. Like the private bathroom, it is impossible to justify on the basis of cost effectiveness, yet imagine the sense of power and importance that arises when one can call a fellow executive on the phone and say, "Fred, I want to take a look at that site you are suggesting for the new widget plant. Meet me there at eleven. I'll fly down in my jet so that I can be back here in the office by seven for the dinner meeting with the board of directors."

The AMA found that 34.3 percent of the companies in the survey reported the availability of a corporate aircraft. In most cases the use of the corporate plane was restricted to the top three levels of management. Ten percent of the companies even allowed personal use of the plane, but two out of three who did so charged for such use. Three-quarters of those who charged for personal use did it on a fixed rate, using either mileage or time as the multiplying factor. The other companies simply calculated the cost of first-class air travel and charged the employee on that basis. However, if the plane was making a business trip, many companies allowed an empty seat to be filled by someone on a personal trip. In that situation, only 10 percent of the companies charged for filling the empty seat.

You might inquire into the availability of your company's jet. If empty seats can be filled at no expense, it is a perk well worth using. Aside from the saving in money, a flight in the company jet offers an opportunity for one-upmanship as you casually let it be known that you just got back from Denver with the CEO in the company jet. Don't overdo this ploy. A single remark in the right place at the right time is much more effective than announcing your coup to everyone in sight.

A recent trial in Washington, D.C., offers an interesting footnote here. Mr. William Tavoulareas, CEO of the Mobil Oil Corporation, sued the *Washington Post* for libel, claiming the newspaper had caused him mental anguish and great professional embarrassment. Mr. Tavoulareas's lawyer called a trucking executive to the stand to attest formally to the outstanding personal qualities possessed by Mr. Tavoulareas. The witness testified that he had no business or professional association with the Mobil Oil company and simply possessed an unbiased admiration for its CEO. The cross-examination consisted of exactly four questions.

Q: Mr. Hoffman, did you just get into Washington just about an hour ago?
A: About an hour and a half I would think.
Q: Did you come up from Florida?
A: No, I did not.
Q: Where did you come from?
A: Indianapolis.
Q: How did you get from Indianapolis to Washington?
A: On the Mobil corporate jet.

On the evidence, if you do manage to secure passage on the company jet, be prepared to encounter some interesting traveling companions.

The Company Hotel Suite

Frank is an enterprising fellow I have known for some years; his career in data processing has been a model of upward mobility. While not yet thirty-five he was made vice president of a rapidly growing company making minicomputers for business and education. Socially, Frank enjoyed equal success, for although not classically handsome he had a way with the ladies. Frank's principal problem was the cost of his social life. He was earning a handsome income but lunch for two, three or four times a week, and frequent after-hour tête-à-têtes, including the cost of hotel rooms, was leaving little of his income for the ski vacations he fancied each winter. It was with considerable relief that Frank learned of company plans to rent on a full-time basis a suite in one of the finer hotels in town. The suite was to be for top-level executives, of which Frank was one, who needed to stay in town overnight, and for meetings during the day. The daytime meetings were to be with out-of-town customers or for staff meetings away from the interruptions of the office.

The president of the company, who lived in a distant suburb, made most use of the suite, often staying overnight, and had his own key. The only other key was in the possession of the president's secretary, who scheduled access to the suite when it was not in use by the president. Frank soon found that the suite was seldom in use at midday and began escorting his lady friends there for an hour or so of companionship. One morning Frank stopped by the desk of the president's secretary to see whether the suite was available that day and found a temporary replacement there, the secretary having called in ill that day. The replacement knew nothing of the suite and Frank helped her find the calendar on which the use of the suite was scheduled. The suite was free for the entire day, so Frank had his name put down for the period from twelve to two and helped search until the key was found. Frank returned to his office and called a newly smitten inamorata and invited her to join him for a drink at noon. The young lady thought this a splendid suggestion, and the two met for drinks at a quiet spot not far from the hotel.

After twenty minutes and two drinks Frank and his companion entered the private elevator. By the time the door to the suite was reached, much of their clothing was being shed. They rushed through the foyer and plunged into the living area on their way to the bedroom. Arising from the sofa was the company president, chivalrously moving to block from view the young lady behind him, who was struggling to replace her blouse without losing her dignity.

The company president was an understanding fellow and Frank was a valued employee, so later that day they reached an accommodation. Frank was to be allowed access to the suite but only when the key was available directly from the president's secretary. The president would inform the secretary each time he planned to use the suite, even if it were only for an hour. And, just to avoid any possibility of a surprise, a chain lock was installed on the inside of the door to the suite, both Frank and his boss pledging to use it whenever the suite was occupied.

One would like to believe that Frank and his boss are atypical of corporate managers, but one must wonder. Company hotel suites are commonplace among large corporations; The Essex House on Central Park South has almost one hundred leased out. It is hard to see the justification for them on a cost-effectiveness basis; a one-bedroom suite in a first-class hotel can easily cost a company $20,000 to $30,000 a year, and it would seem difficult to justify that as a necessary expense. One must conclude that the function of a corporate suite is to provide another perk for top managers, a goodie that lifts a manager above the herd and reaffirms his status, while offering an opportunity for enhanced social life at minimal cost. Few perks have the kind of double-barrelled attraction that can rival the appeal of a private suite at a fancy hotel.

If your company has a suite and you do not have direct access, perhaps you can use it through the good offices of your boss. The next time you schedule an all-day staff meeting with your people, you might inquire of your boss as to the availability of the suite. If arrangements can be made for you to use it, you will accomplish a number of objectives. First, you will enhance your image in the eyes of your staff. Second, you will elevate your status in the eyes of your peers. Third, you will promote your image as the kind of person who gets things done in innovative ways. And fourth, you demonstrate your fitness to use a perk reserved for those higher up. All those factors will count in your favor when it comes time to appoint the next company vice president. When that day arrives and the suite becomes available to you on your own recognizance, remember the tale of Frank and his lady friend; your own president or another executive might not be so understanding as Frank's boss. The protocol upon entering a corporate suite is as follows:

1. Knock loudly upon the door or ring the bell repeatedly. Do not let your eagerness prompt you into a hasty entrance; remember, many senior executives have diminished hearing and slower reaction times.
2. Upon opening the door, announce your presence in a voice sufficiently loud to be heard without difficulty in the farthest corner of the bedroom.
3. Walk into all rooms, announcing your approach in advance.
4. If there is no chain, bring a small, triangular rubber doorstop to slip under the door on the inside.

Following these simple rules, you will avoid embarrassment and demonstrate to all that you know how the game is played.

The Executive Dining Room

Many corporations have set aside special dining rooms available only to their top managers. There, in quiet, tasteful surroundings, one can dine among peers in the certain knowledge that at the next table will not be a fellow in his shirtsleeves uttering coarse comments to the waitress as he swigs down a Dr. Pepper straight from the bottle. The executive dining room is almost always located on the top floor of the corporate offices, with large windows to give those inside the sense of importance that comes from looking down on the ant-sized figures of their fellow men. (For some reason, Mobil Oil has its dining room for middle managers located in the basement.) The walls are usually paneled in dark wood, the carpeting thick but dull in color, and the wall decorations expensively framed reproductions of nautical scenes. Any exception to standard decor is probably the work of the much-younger second wife of the chairman of the board who spent a year as an apprentice window trimmer at Bloomingdale's. Under those circumstances the executive dining room will have the bright, cheery appearance of a pediatrician's office. The walls will be painted an off-shade of yellow and the carpeting will have been replaced by large, multicolored tiles imported from Italy. The wall decorations will be original tapestry works of irregular size and puzzling design done by some fantastic young artist down in the Village. The solid-wood tables and chairs will have been replaced with examples of the latest development in the art of shaping quarter-inch polystyrene.

Whatever the decor, those dining will be genial but soft-spoken. The unwritten rule is that all company disputes are checked at the door, like six-guns at a mining camp bordello. Aside from slurping soup, the most serious breach of manners is to raise one's voice or inject emotion into a discussion. Conversation must be conducted in the stately tones and measured cadence of a mortician asking the necessary details for a death notice. Humor is acceptable only if dry and understated, preferably in the style of the late Harold Macmillan. Prepared jokes, especially with a smutty content, are certain to bring clucks of disapproval. The jollying of waitresses is unthinkable since they will all be middle-aged and wearing support hose. Table-hopping is frowned upon, for it gives the appearance of company politicking. It is, however, acceptable upon departure to stop briefly at another table to set up a meeting with a peer or subordinate. Never approach a superior in this manner.

The exceptions to these rules of conduct are to be found in southern California, of course, where the slurping of soup will go unnoticed amid the roar of vulgarities emanating from every table. Instead of brief, manly handshakes there will be huggings and back-poundings and cries of "Baby!" and "Sweetheart!" as the diners hop from one table to another, wheeling, dealing, promoting, and politicking. The decor will be Hollywood Modern with much use of track lighting. In recognition of the dining habits of southern Californians, the walls and floors will be of washable material.

Regardless of location, do not expect much from the chef. The food will be edible but far below the standards of the Cunard Line or your neighborhood trattoria. No matter how strongly you are importuned to do otherwise, never have more than one glass of wine. Remember, you are not there to dine well or enjoy yourself; you are there to see and be seen, to mingle with the great and the near-great, and to confirm your status as one of the nobles of the realm.

The AMA found 127 companies, or 17.4 percent of those responding, who provide special dining arrangements for their executives. A single dining facility was used for the top management group in seventy-eight companies, and thirty-six of them actually included middle managers. Those thirty-six companies must be located in remote desert areas where no other food is available, or else they have no understanding of the purpose of an executive dining room. What is the sense in having an exclusive dining facility that is not exclusive? They might just as well expand their cafeterias and let everyone eat together in the spirit of participatory democracy.

Twenty-nine firms reported having separate dining rooms for different levels of management. Now that's more like it! With those companies you have something to look forward to; each time you get a promotion you join a more exclusive group of dining partners. There are twenty other companies that carry that process to its logical conclusion: they provide individual dining rooms for their top officers. There you have it, the ultimate dining perk: eating alone!

Seventy-two companies provided information on the policy they follow in pricing meals in their executive dining rooms:

Above cost	7 companies
At cost	19 companies
Below cost	15 companies
At no charge	31 companies

It's hard to fathom the reasoning of the seven companies that are making a profit on their executive dining room. One wonders whether the serfs using the cafeterias in those companies are also paying above cost for their meals. If not, it would seem that legal action is in order to remedy this flagrant discrimination. Ralph Nader, where are you when we need you?

The Private Dining Club

There are of course many companies, especially those occupying space in large office buildings, that provide no dining facilities for any of their employees. In those situations, and frequently even when the company has its own executive dining room, companies will often pay the cost of membership in private dining clubs for selected executives. The cost of such memberships ranges from $500 a year on up to many thousands, depending upon the exclusiveness of the club and its desirability as a place to meet the movers and shakers of the world. You are of course also charged for all meals and drinks taken at the club, but often the monthly charges are sent directly to the company and you need not concern yourself with them. Most dining clubs are open for both lunch and dinner and have a minimum monthly charge that is assessed whether or not you use the club.

The AMA found that 59.8 percent of the companies surveyed paid dues for their executives in luncheon or supper clubs. Banking and financial institutions led the field in providing this perk, with 78.6 percent offering the perk to CEOs, 60.7 percent to corporate officers, 39.3 percent to top management, and 10.7 percent to middle managers. Most of my banking friends have formed eating groups and rotate their luncheon meetings among the clubs of the group members so that no one ever has to pay for a lunch. Much of the lunchtime discussion is focused on how to reduce the waistlines produced by daily ingestion of Chicken Kiev, Veal Cordon Bleu, Fettucine Alfredo, and Beef Bourguignonne.

The existence of private dining and social clubs apparently represents a threat to the American Way of Life, at least to the House of Delegates of the American Bar Association. That august body in January of 1982 voted to ask that the Civil Rights Act of 1964 be extended to cover private clubs. Apparently it has come to the attention of the lawyers that business (ooh, that dirty word!) is occasionally discussed at private clubs. The House of Delegates reasons from that as follows:

1. Not all clubs are open to anyone who might wish to join.
2. Nonmembers are unable to participate in business discussions occurring in private clubs.
3. Women, blacks, and other minorities who are not club members are unfairly handicapped in their efforts to advance in their business careers.
4. Therefore, private clubs should be abolished or opened to all.

There is of course no way for the ABA delegates to know how much business is actually conducted in private clubs or to be able to prove that not being present at such discussions is a handicap to someone in business. The delegates have proposed a test to determine whether a club is primarily for social or business purposes: "If 20 percent or more of a club's revenues have been treated as business expenses for tax purposes, then sufficient business is conducted at the club to warrant prohibiting discrimination by the club." How the 20 percent figure was arrived at was not described by the delegates, but one must assume that it is a demonstration of the traditional lawyer's skill at creating a cause for action out of nothing.

My first exposure to private dining clubs came while I was still young and dismally inexperienced in the ways of the business world. I joined a small Chicago company to start a venture that offered an opportunity for the company to move into a new market area. The president of the company was interested in the potential of the new venture, and one morning my boss told me that the president would like to have us join him for lunch and learn more about my activities. At noon we met in the lobby and I was introduced to the president, breathing deeply and evenly to calm my nerves. It was a lovely morning in June, and a taxi quickly deposited the three of us at 333 N. Michigan Avenue where an elevator whisked us to the top floor and the hushed precincts of the Tavern Club. A black-clad maître d' groveled us to a table by the window where we could look west along the Chicago River.

My superiors immediately ordered Bloody Marys and I followed suit, not having the independence of mind to order something different. My drinking experience at that time consisted solely of a devotion to Fox DeLuxe Beer and I had no knowledge of the ingredients in a Bloody Mary. I was pleased with the tangy tomato flavor of the drink and quaffed it eagerly. It seemed an adequate replacement for my customary breakfast with juice, which I had skipped that morning, and I assumed that the other two men had also missed their morning juice. When the president, who was still sipping his, politely asked whether I would like another Bloody Mary, I acquiesced with a smiling nod.

Our luncheon orders followed the previous pattern in that the president ordered Welsh rarebit and neither my boss nor I saw fit to order anything different. The president asked me to describe my activities and where I saw the new venture leading us. My face was flushed as I began my recital, but I attributed my condition to a failure of the air-conditioning system, although it did not appear my tablemates were bothered by the heat.

Lunch arrived and it was with some surprise that I saw a plate of warm cheese on toast placed in front of me. I accepted the strange meal as one of the ways in which top business executives differed from me and momentarily wondered what other differences existed of which I was not yet aware. Fortunately, lunch came with another Bloody Mary for each of us, a welcome boon to my dry throat. My recitation was now in full flight and I dared not stop to eat for fear of losing my place, but frequent draughts of drink were necessary to ease a thirst induced by nervousness. My monologue continued as I became aware of a strange lightness in the air, but I plunged on with the dogged persistence of Sisyphus.

Sometime later, a period that I subsequently estimated to be six or seven minutes, I experienced a sensation hitherto confined to long stretches on a highway when I suddenly realized I couldn't remember the previous few minutes. I discovered that I was leaning toward the president with my arm about his neck and heard myself, as if from a distance, describing the manifold shortcomings of the company and how they might be corrected. I stopped abruptly as my boss and the president sat frozen in their chairs, positions that I realized they had been holding for some minutes. I removed my arm from the president's neck, my last, unfinished sentence seeming to hang in the air, and turned to the study of my Welsh rarebit with great intensity.

The rest of that meal is mercifully only a blur in my memory, but I do recall the others covering my abrupt silence with some strained remarks about the weather and, much later, walking from the table to the elevator with the slow, stately gait of a stork crossing a shallow pond. Neither of my luncheon companions ever referred to that afternoon, but there were no future invitations to dine with the president; to this day I cannot enter a private dining club without a reaction once described by S. J. Perelman: "My neck, usually an alabaster column, began to turn a dull, brick red."

A Reserved Parking Place

Near where I live is a building that houses some equipment for part of the city transportation system. The equipment is self-contained, requiring little maintenance but frequent visits by the engineering staff to check its condition. During their visits the engineers have been in the habit of parking indiscriminately along a wall of the building. There is room for four cars and there are only four engineers who visit, so parking is not a problem. Last week I noticed large signs painted on the wall designating assigned parking areas:

			CHIEF
ENGINEER	ENGINEER	ENGINEER	ENGINEER

The chief engineer's parking spot was closest to the entry door, fully thirty feet closer than the farthest spot, and I had to admire the chief's insistence on all the perks of his position, no matter how minor.

Many company parking lots have the area nearest the entrance reserved for corporate officers. This saves the half-mile walk from the far reaches of the lot but deprives them of much-needed exercise. However, on a day of driving rain it is comforting for the CEO and his top aides to know that they will enter the office crisp and dry—at least relatively so, since even the executive parking area can be forty or fifty yards from the entrance. Some companies have solved this problem by providing sheltered parking places for their top people, which also lessens the buildup of heat inside the vehicles during hot, sunny days.

Reserved parking places give lower level managers a daily incentive reminder of what lies ahead for them if they apply themselves diligently to their work. It is not just the reserved parking place that is so enticing but the vehicles which occupy them. The unspoken message is, "Someday you too can drive a Lincoln Continental and have a special parking place for it." Of course, this message can only be transmitted if the CEO and his vice presidents arrive before and leave after the other managers.

There is one negative aspect to having a reserved parking place: It makes your vehicle an easy target for disgruntled employees. A friend of mine, a plant manager for a large manufacturing concern, has learned to park his car in an anonymous spot in the lot on the day he plans to terminate someone; the trips to a windshield replacement service were becoming time consuming.

The AMA found that a reserved parking place was the most common perk provided to corporate executives, with 76 percent of the companies offering it to at least one level of management. Almost 34 percent of the companies provided sheltered spaces for one or more levels of management. Banking and financial institutions were most considerate in this respect: 71.4 percent of them provided sheltered space for the CEO. The wholesale and retail trades lagged far behind, with only 25 percent providing sheltered spaces.

By now you have probably discerned the essential purpose of perks relating to status: They do not exist to provide money or time or pleasure but to separate anointed executives from the proletariat. The separation has three purposes. First, it confirms to the executive that he is someone special, that, though he can be discharged on a moment's notice for a downturn in sales or productivity, he is nevertheless a person of importance who has "made it." Second, it makes the everyday life of the executive somewhat easier, to compensate for the constant pressure on him to improve upon last year's performance. Third, it creates an aura about those who are separated by their never being seen engaged in ordinary activities. The aura of differentness enhances the power and adds to the prestige of an executive.

The creation of an executive aura needs elaboration. A corporate CEO is much like the captain of a ship, with responsibility for charting a course and directing the activities of the crew. In order for the ship (or corporation) to function effectively the crew must have confidence in their captain and believe that his decisions will benefit them. The crew must feel that the captain knows his job and that he will lead them to a safe harbor. A wise captain enhances this feeling by not mingling indiscriminately with the crew, by issuing his orders in a calm decisive manner, and by never showing doubt as to what the next course of action should be. It is no accident that his followers referred to

Mao Tse-tung as "The Great Helmsman"; he was the man steering their country, supposedly toward a better life for all. Both Mao and Charles de Gaulle created about themselves an aura of Olympian omniscience by not involving themselves in the day-to-day problems of their countries and by reserving their public appearances for special occasions. The French and Chinese, awed by the aura surrounding their great leaders, responded by according them a respect and obedience not given to their other political figures, and both France and China enjoyed an unaccustomed stability, at least for a time.

Part of the aura of a successful politician or corporate leader is created by the need to find a father figure in whom we can repose our trust. We want to believe that whoever is in charge of our fate is a special person who will take care of us as well as our fathers did when we were children. Much of the aura of Franklin Roosevelt was a result of his deliberate effort to appear a calm, confident father figure who had the answers to our nation's problems. In corporate life we bestow these same virtues upon our company CEO, seeing him as competent, far-sighted, and able to handle the competition. We relax, feeling we are in good hands, and turn to our work with confidence. This confidence in our CEO is automatically given by us because we need to feel we are well looked after, whether or not the CEO is deserving of our confidence. If the CEO acts and speaks with confidence and assurance, he will continue to have our confidence and the aura of his position will work to his advantage. His suggestions and commands will be obeyed without hesitation and the company will become a powerful, flexible instrument of his will. All of which is to the good so long as the CEO is truly capable and far-sighted.

If a CEO has been successful in creating a powerful aura, his possessions take on a power of their own. At one time CBS managers could arrange for a tiptoe visit to the private office of William Paley when the great man was out of town. They would stand huddled in the entrance, scarcely daring to enter, content just to stare wide-eyed at the very desk where He did His work, at the telephone He actually talked into and the chair He actually sat in! A suggestion was once made that one of the visitors might like to sit in the chair behind the desk. A look of horror and shock crossed the visitor's face and he visibly trembled at the thought of such desecration.

The presence of a great leader can lend distinction to an otherwise ordinary place through the retention of his aura; even now there are inns and homes in the East whose claim to fame is that "George Washington slept here." The boyhood homes of our presidents are carefully preserved so we can see with our own eyes their actual possessions, the floors they walked upon, and the beds they slept in.

Even the names of our leaders take on a magical cast; as with the ancient Hebrews who dared not speak the name of the Almighty and used Jehovah as a *nom de dieu,* corporate CEOs are often referred to indirectly. We speak of "the Old Man" or "J.B." or "the Big Guy" or that straight-talk holdover from the nineteenth century, "The Boss." At some companies the CEO's aura is so powerful that even those terms are too familiar-sounding and the great man is designated by location: "I hope we can get the thirty-fifth floor to buy off on this."

An aura that powerful is not created by having the CEO work out of a cubicle with glass sides making him visible to all, by watching him drive into the company lot in his six-year-old Chevy, by seeing him in line in the company cafeteria each noontime, and by standing next to him in the men's room. An effective CEO aura is created by distance, both physical and psychological. Creating that distance and enhancing the aura of top managers is a primary raison d'être for the perks of status.

— 11 —

Perks and the Independent Business Person

Of course, the world of perks is not confined to large corporations. Sole owners of businesses and self-employed individuals—ranging from my junk-dealing friends in the bleachers at Wrigley Field to doctors, lawyers, and accountants—have a plethora of perks available to them. The important distinction between perks provided by a company to an employee and perks for a self-employed person is that the self-employed person is using his own money. However, a perk is by definition a business expense and therefore the cost is shared with the Internal Revenue Service. As a self-employed individual enjoys the perks of independence, he can be comforted by the thought that up to half their cost will be returned to him in the form of a tax deduction. For many, this knowledge provides an extra fillip of satisfaction.

The tax laws have been revised so that the owner of a small business can have the earnings reported as personal income. This avoids the double taxation of paying a business tax and a personal tax and keeps the maximum tax rate at 50 percent. On that basis, then, the cost of any perk to an independent business person is usually 50 percent of the actual amount.

A great advantage enjoyed by an independent business person is that no one's permission is needed in the granting of a perk; no boss or board of directors must approve it. The self-employed person is free to grant whatever perks are desired, and the time thus saved undoubtedly helps contribute to the high productivity of small businesses.

The disadvantage for an independent business person, aside from the fact that he is paying for at least half the cost, is that the IRS will look more closely at the perk than if he were a corporate employee. The IRS reasons, in most cases quite correctly, that corporations control the dispensation of perks so that employees are not enjoying unwarranted tax advantages. Those built-in controls do not exist for an independent business person, and the IRS looks quite carefully at deductions claimed by self-employed persons. Therefore, the proper use of perks for an independent business person involves a constant consideration of the IRS stance on individual perks. Self-employed persons who are ignorant of IRS rulings or who choose to ignore them will soon discover themselves in tax courts, where deductions will be disallowed for yachts, landscaping of private homes, personal travel, imaginative pension plans, club memberships under the guise of medical expenses, and other creative schemes to enjoy life at the expense of the government.

The self-employed person who is tax-wise will shift as many of his ordinary living expenses to his business without incurring the suspicion, let alone the wrath, of the IRS. Accomplishing this almost always requires consultation with a knowledgeable accountant or tax attorney, and such consultation should occur before acquiring the perk.

Let's see what a self-employed person need do to enjoy some of the good things in life without developing a close personal relationship with members of the Internal Revenue Service. It should be noted that all suggestions are based on IRS rulings as of this writing. Rulings in individual cases can vary considerably from one IRS district to another, so the suggestions should not be considered as reflecting a consistency in IRS practices that does not exist in fact. Moreover, IRS rulings change, and what was acceptable yesterday is often no longer acceptable today. The only safe course is to view these suggestions as nothing more than that and to consult with a tax adviser before taking specific action on a perk.

A Company Car

This is one perk that the IRS almost never questions. Even if you are a freelance writer of greeting-card poems and never leave your apartment because your African violets need constant attention, you are entitled to an automobile to assist you in your work. Not only that, there is no restriction on the cost of the vehicle. It can be a Cadillac or a Rolls-Royce and can even come with a driver; if you want to spend that much money, the IRS will not call you on it. If, however, your company vehicle is a Formula I racing car best suited to the banked turns at Le Mans, the IRS may well question it as an essential tool of your trade.

The IRS may also ask how much the car is used for personal purposes. If it is the only automobile in the family, you will have to assign some percentage of its use to personal affairs. The usual allocation for personal use is between 10 and 20 percent, which means that only 80 to 90 percent of the total operating cost and depreciation can be taken as a deduction. The same percentage would apply to costs of parking the car and the various fees attached to its use.

Entertaining at Home

Moderation is the key element here, as well as in many of the other perks available to the self-employed person. A dinner party once or twice a month in which at least one business guest is present will pass unnoticed. Receipts for all food and beverages should be retained, and the cost of temporary help to prepare, serve, and clean up afterwards should be documented. Tax court files are filled with tales of deductions for business entertainment at home that turned out to be Sweet-Sixteen celebrations paid for by a doting father, or similar nonbusiness occasions. One must remember that when a deduction is disallowed and evidence exists that deliberate deception was used, not only is the amount of the original tax due but there are interest and penalties that can frequently double or triple the sum owed.

A Liberal Expense Account

The general rule here is to write off all that you can, but keep records and receipts so every expense can be documented if necessary. If you are questioned, your records simply attest to the fact that the people with whom you do business have a great interest in sporting events, the ballet and the opera, opening nights at the theatre, afternoons at the country club, piano bars, and expensive restaurants. In order to qualify as a legitimate deduction there must be some business discussion at some point during the outing. The discussion need not be prolonged or conclusive, but something about business should be said. In addition, if the outing immediately followed a business meeting it is not essential that business be discussed at the outing; all that is required is that the outing be a logical extension of the business meeting.

Extra Vacation Time

The irony of self-employment is that often the money is available for frequent or extended vacations but there is little time to take them. A professional, such as a lawyer or doctor, will find that the demands of clients and patients prevent more than a week or two away from the office each

211

year. The owner of a small business will seldom have someone to whom the business can be entrusted while he's away on an extended cruise of the Greek Isles. The perk is there, but it's only available to those who can plan for it and make a deliberate effort to use it. If you own a small business, you will need a trusted lieutenant who can manage the enterprise in your absence; this means that you must spend considerable time training that person. Breaking free on a regular basis from your own business or practice is not easy, but if you can't enjoy some of life why are you making all that money?

Overseas Travel

Once you've decided to get away from it all, there is no sense in personally bearing the entire cost of your travels. It is all but impossible for someone to be engaged in a profession or business and not find a legitimate business tie-in to a trip overseas. There are conventions, workshops, meetings, seminars, expositions, and fairs, any one of which can serve as a business reason for the trip. If all else fails, there is always the educational survey to discover how others in your profession or business are handling problems similar to yours. The business part of the trip may only take a day or so, but at least you can deduct the cost of the air fare and a day or two of hotel bills and meal expenses. Let the IRS share in a legitimate portion of your travel expenses; it'll make the dinner tab at Le Tour D'Argent seem much more palatable.

First-class Air Travel

You can be sure that the director of the Internal Revenue Service travels first class, and there is no reason why you shouldn't, too. The IRS will utter no protest, even if you spend $1,800 to take the Concorde to London or Paris. Let's face it, if it weren't for business travelers from the

United States, the British and French would have long since had to shut down the Concorde service, taking losses in the billions of dollars, which ultimately would have caused severe strains on the North Atlantic Treaty Alliance. If your business can afford it, go first class—you've made it; now it's time to enjoy it!

Special Hotel Accommodations

The same principle applies to your hotel rooms. If you can afford it, there is no reason to stay anywhere except the best places—and in suites, not rooms. Why settle for anything less? Until you have been ushered into a sumptuous hotel suite and have looked down on the huddled masses from your fortieth-floor window while the butler hangs up your duds and pours a glass of wine, you will not have experienced the full sensation of having made it.

Spouse's Travel

Taking your spouse with you on a business trip is not a problem; getting the IRS to accept the additional expense as business-related is a bit more difficult. The safest course is to have your spouse in attendance at all or most of the business meetings you conduct. Your spouse then becomes a partner in your work whose advice and counsel you find indispensable. This may present a problem if you are in a licensed profession—law, medicine, plumbing, etc.—and your spouse does not possess professional credentials. In such instances, if your spouse is a man, his presence might be justified on the basis of providing personal security for you and carrying luggage and equipment. If you're a man, your wife might take notes during meetings and provide you with a written record of your discussions. Whatever the justification for the spouse's presence, it should be decided upon ahead of time and the trip conducted accordingly. Do not wait until you have returned home and then decide to justify your spouse's presence; no matter how carefully you reconstruct things it is all but impossible to make it ring true to the IRS.

Airline VIP Clubs

If your business or profession requires regular air travel, by all means join at least one of these clubs. The services they provide are well worth the nominal cost and, again, it's all tax deductible.

Country Clubs

The IRS has been getting more and more difficult to satisfy when it comes to club memberships for independent business people. They will not allow a deduction for the initial cost of a membership, since that is regarded as an asset that can be sold to another prospective member. Special assessments to improve the clubhouse or add tennis courts or similar improvements are also usually not deductible. Monthly fees, either as direct charges or as minimums, are deductible in proportion to your business use of the club. In other words, if you use the club 30 percent of the time for business purposes, then 30 percent of the monthly fees would be deductible. Any business entertaining you do at the club is 100-percent deductible, whether it is for a round of golf, dinner in the clubhouse, or drinks at the bar. If you pay guest fees for your business associates or their families, those costs are also deductible. The reality of club memberships is that it is difficult to write off more than a small portion of the total cost of your membership. However, if you would be a club member even if there were no write-offs at all, then every little bit helps.

Private Yacht or Hunting Lodge

There is almost no way the IRS is going to allow you to deduct more than a very small portion of the operating costs of these possessions as business-related. The IRS reasons that a corporation owning such property has a large number of executives who can make a legitimate business use of the yacht or the lodge. They do not feel that a lone independent business person can spend enough time on the yacht or at the lodge to justify more than a minimal tax write-off. If you can't afford to bear the whole cost, forget the idea—tax write-offs will not make it financially feasible.

Your Office

Have you dreamed of surrounding yourself with the opulent splendor of Suleiman the Magnificent? If you've got the money, go ahead: The Tax laws place no effective restraint on spending for the design and furnishings of your office. After all, it's your work environment, and who is to say that a $4,000 Bokhara carpet is not essential to the serenity of mind needed to properly manage your business? Marble coffee tables, sofas covered in raw silk, solid mahogany desks and credenzas, teakwood floors, linen wall coverings, expensive European drapes, silver coffee sets, and lighting designed by Tharon Musser can all be considered legitimate business expenses. You probably spend more time in your office than at home, so why not make it as pleasant as possible? One note of caution: Works of art are considered tangible assets and cannot be written off as business expenses even if they are physically located in your office. In addition, works of art cannot be depreciated; the IRS assumes that they are probably actually increasing in value. If when they are sold you incur a loss, you can then deduct the loss from that year's income.

If your office is in your home, you still need not stint, and you can also deduct a proportional share of the rent, light, insurance, and heating costs. If the office is in a home or apartment you own, though, you cannot deduct anything for the monthly mortgage payments, and since you are already entitled to a 100-percent deduction for taxes and interest, there isn't much left to write off. However, you can still deduct a proportional share of the operating costs of the property—heat, light, insurance, snow removal, painting, window washing, cleaning, etc.

The IRS has gotten increasingly sticky about in-home offices, and the requirements for qualification are much more strict than they used to be. A desk with a file drawer in a corner of the living room no longer qualifies as an office. In order to deduct the expenses of an in-home office, the office should be in a separate room that is not used for nonbusiness purposes; a television set in the room automatically causes it to be suspect. This does not mean that overnight guests who occasionally sleep on the office couch will cause you to lose your deduction; however, a family member who slumbers there nightly will provoke a sharp response from the IRS.

A Private Secretary

Great leeway exists in the hiring of a private secretary for an independent business person. The secretary can be male or female, attractive as well as efficient, young or old, English-speaking or not, and the pay and duties are whatever the two of you agree upon. All the costs of the secretary are tax deductible. This includes whatever equipment and furniture is supplied to make the secretary more productive or more comfortable. If you find the contribution of your secretary to your work effectiveness and physical well-being is well above the norm and you decide to provide a salary of $50,000 per year in appreciation, the IRS must accept the pay as justified. The pay of your secretary and the duties expected are entirely between the two of you, and this includes whatever perks you wish to grant the secretary. So long as the duties and perks are business-related, the total costs of your secretary are deductible as business expenses.

Private Hotel Suite

If you live near but not in a city, and if you conduct considerable business in the city without having an office there, you may be able to justify the cost of a permanent hotel suite as a business expense. To qualify, the suite must be used primarily for business purposes. Your business meetings must be conducted there and guests who stay overnight should have a business relationship with you. Your own overnight stays should either be in preparation for a next day's business meeting or because a business affair lasted into the evening and it was too late to return to your home outside the city. Whatever entertaining you do in the suite should be business-related, which necessitates at least one guest who has a business relationship with you. The IRS may still want to know how much of the time the suite is used for nonbusiness purposes, and you should have documentation to prove the extent of the suite's business use.

A Private Airplane

The IRS cannot compel you to fly on commercial airlines or patronize Amtrak. If you choose to do your business traveling in your private airplane, that is your prerogative. The cost of the plane and its operating costs then become legitimate business deductions, as are the cost of a pilot and expenses for ground maintenance. If you also use the plane for pleasure or personal travel, the IRS will expect that only the proportional share of the plane's expenses be deducted from your business income.

Keogh Plans

One of the most substantial benefits to being self-employed is the ability to significantly reduce your current taxable income and simultaneously set aside funds for your retirement. The principal vehicle is a Keogh Plan, named for a New York congressman, who was concerned that self-employed individuals might end up on the welfare rolls after retirement and persuaded the Congress to take action. In brief, a Keogh Plan allows a self-employed person to put money into a retirement fund and deduct the amount from his current taxable income.

For example, in 1983 a self-employed person with an earned income of $100,000 can place $15,000 into a Keogh Plan account. His taxable income would be reduced so that he would only pay taxes on $85,000. While the money is in a Keogh Plan account, any interest or dividend earned is also not taxed, so the compounding effect is greatly enhanced.

Until 1981 the maximum amount that could be deposited into a Keogh Plan account in any one year was $7,500. The formula for determining contributions was 15 percent of earned income up to a maximum earned income of $50,000. For calendar years 1982 and 1983 the maximum contribution was increased to $15,000 by raising the earned income ceiling to $100,000. For calendar year 1984 two significant changes will occur:

1. The percentage of earned income that may be set aside will increase to 25 percent.
2. The maximum contribution will be raised to $30,000.

This means that beginning in 1984 a self-employed person with $120,000 of earned income will be able to set aside 25 percent of income, or $30,000, into a Keogh Plan account and reduce the taxable income to $90,000. On a smaller scale, a person with an earned income of $60,000 will be able to shelter up to $15,000 of income in a Keogh Plan account. Please note that in computing "earned income" you cannot include interest or dividends received, inheritances, sweepstakes prizes, or other sources of income that are not a direct result of your labors.

Of course, as the Congress giveth, so the Congress taketh away: The money is not exempt from taxes forever. All payments into Keogh Plans and accumulations of interest and dividends will eventually be subject to taxation. When money is paid out of a Keogh Plan account, it is added to whatever income you have at that time and taxed at your regular rates. The assumption is that money will not be received from a Keogh Plan account until you have retired and are, presumably, in a lower tax bracket.

Money cannot be withdrawn without penalty from a Keogh Plan account until age 59½. If money is withdrawn before that age, the regular tax is paid on the amount withdrawn and a 10-percent penalty is added on.

If a self-employed person has employees, they must be included in whatever Keogh Plan is established. The only requirement for the employees is that they have at least three years of service and work full time, which usually means at least 1,000 hours per year. You must contribute to an employee's plan in the same percentage that you contribute to your plan. As a reward for contributing to Keogh Plans for your employees, you are allowed to add up to $2,500 voluntarily to your own Keogh Plan account. The voluntary contributions are not tax deductible, but the interest or dividends they earn is. Moreover, voluntary contributions may be withdrawn at any time without penalty. Most Keogh Plan monies are deposited with banks, insurance companies, mutual funds, stockbrokers, or other organizations that can operate as fiduciary trustees. Such organizations have done all the legal work and preparation of forms necessary to establish a Keogh Plan and will be happy to discuss the establishment of a plan with you.

It is also possible for a self-employed person with substantial income to shelter more than $30,000 per year in a Keogh Plan account under a Defined Benefit Plan. This would be used instead of the Defined Contribution Plan, which was described above. The requirements for a Defined Benefit Plan and its operation are so complex that it is not possible to describe them properly here. To establish a Defined Benefit Plan or modify a current Defined Contribution plan so that it becomes one you should consult a tax attorney experienced in this field.

One final note. If you have a Keogh Plan, you can still have an IRA and deposit up to $2,000 each year into it. Deposits into an IRA are also tax deductible, and essentially the same rules apply for withdrawals as with a Keogh Plan.

— 12 —

Perk-Man

It's a little known fact that the video game Pac-Man was designed as a replication of the life of a perks player. Each little perk that is gobbled up represents one small but important gain for Perk-Man. Each perk successfully swallowed makes Perk-Man stronger and more capable of escaping the evil forces determined to end his career. Perk-Man must stay in constant motion, ever alert to the changing conditions of the game. Danger can come from any angle and allies can unexpectedly turn into enemies. Yet even while remaining vigilant, the search for perks must continue, for it is the accumulation of perks that provides the strength Perk-Man needs to compete effectively. Although a rest would often be welcome, the game must go on; the pursuit of perks cannot cease for in the perks lies the only hope of survival for Perk-Man. Perk-Man must know the intentions, capabilities, and strategies of his pursuers. He must know his own strengths and weaknesses and those of his opponents. He must turn his understanding of the game to his advantage: how to hide momentarily from pursuers, how to avoid being trapped, how to change swiftly from flight to attack, how to acquire only those perks that are truly helpful and ignore those that can lead to disaster.

The life of Perk-Man is not an easy one, but it is the only game in town and should therefore be played with zest and confidence. A steady eye and confident hand are required; there is no place for doubt or hesitation, for those are the afflictions of life's losers. The game goes on and the score mounts ever higher for those who can stay the route. The rewards are there, but they will not be won by those too faint-hearted to try or those who give less than their best effort.

When the game is over and you step away from the arena, leave a score on the board next to your name so that those who follow will say, *"There* was a player!"

Index